The Art of Being an Intellectual

# THE ART OF BEING

# AN INTELLECTUAL

## by Ignace Lepp

Translated by Bernard Murchland

THE MACMILLAN COMPANY, NEW YORK

First published in France under
title of *L'Art de Vivre de L'Intellectuel*
by Editions Universitaires, Paris.

*First Printing*

The Macmillan Company, New York
Collier-Macmillan Ltd., Toronto, Ontario
PRINTED IN THE UNITED STATES OF AMERICA

# Contents

v

*13859*

# *Preface*

This book is intended as a practical guide for intellectuals in the second half of the twentieth century. Thus it will not be primarily concerned with ideological or theoretical issues.

I should like to begin, then, by outlining my subject matter and defining that existential entity called an *intellectual*. Let me say straight away that I in no way consider him a superman. My book is not addressed to supermen but to the increasing number of educated men and women who are interested in the life of the mind, who are or want to become intellectuals. Such persons are not necessarily superior to the rest of the human race. It is true that an intellectual is generally better educated; but other men may excel by reason of their moral and spiritual character or their achievements in the field of action and art. Many saints, like Francis of Assisi, were in no sense of the word intellectuals; yet they contributed mightily to the progress of human history. In the twentieth century, which is so proud of its intellectual achievements, a man so universally admired as Pope John was not an intellectual.

Thus this book on the "art of being an intellectual" is not

motivated by any kind of caste pride; I am not claiming any special rank or privilege for intellectuals. They are not in my mind a new aristocracy; many of them are quite frankly inferior to men in other walks of life. Among intellectuals there are saints and sinners as well as a large number of "average" men.

Nonetheless, the intellectual has certain specific characteristics; life confronts him with special problems; and he has a unique social function. Like any human life his should be productive, although this term need not be interpreted in a narrow spatial or temporal sense. Many of the remarks we direct to intellectuals will also be applicable to other men, for intellectuals are not walled off from the rest of the human race. As we shall see, it is not always easy to determine whether or not a given individual belongs to the *intelligentsia*.

I am especially concerned to reach the young intellectuals. Among high school and university students many, both by temperament and talent, are capable of becoming very competent intellectuals, and some of them will make original and creative contributions. But unless they know how to use their talents effectively they will waste them. I have known young students who gave every promise of brilliant futures; but ten years later they were mediocre bourgeois. If what I have to say, based on my own experience as an intellectual as well as the experience of the many people I have counseled, can in any way reduce such a waste of talent my efforts will have been amply rewarded.

The spiritual masters teach that if one wants to become a saint he must begin by becoming a man in the fullest sense of the word. The same is true for the intellectual. It may be objected that in the case of the saint grace supplies for the imperfections of nature while no such grace is available for the intellectual—unless some sort of analogy is postulated between grace in the supernatural order and genius in the natural order. But genius is rare, and in any event we are not writing for geniuses in these pages. Intellectuals cannot limit their effort to acquiring and assimilating knowledge and developing their cerebral capacities to the maximum. Juvenal's celebrated maxim still holds: *mens sana in corpore sano* (a healthy mind in a healthy body).

Intellectual efficacy depends largely on one's general state of well-being. Thus the reader should not be surprised that we consecrate several pages to body hygiene, diet, and the different methods of rest and relaxation. The limits of this book will not permit us to enter into any great detail, however. For the most part we shall indicate general principles and refer the reader to more technical works for details.

Emotional health is quite as important as physical health. There are men whose whole lives are caught up in intellectual passion, men who need neither love nor friendship to be happy. But they are a minority. For most intellectuals the choice between celibacy or marriage, chastity or license, as well as relations with friends, teachers, and disciples raise real existential problems. The quality of intellectual work itself is often conditioned by emotional health, but it is not always easy to reconcile the two. We shall discuss the principal dangers that threaten harmony between the mind and the heart as well as the means by which they might be overcome. Intellectuals are especially susceptible to certain forms of neuroses. It is important to be able to recognize and remedy them.

Female intellectuals also have special problems. Some thinkers are of the opinion that they can be intellectuals only at the cost of renouncing their femininity. While recognizing the difficulties in this case, we think that they can be resolved.

Finally, we shall have to discuss the relationship between

the intellectual life and religious faith. Obviously some people never have this problem. But others believe or want to believe in God and belong or want to belong to a Church, but are often hard put to harmonize their faith with the demands of their intellectual vocation. Perhaps what I have to say will be of some help to such harmony.

In the modern world almost all intellectuals, like other members of the community, exercise a profession. Choice of such a profession is not easy. We have to bear in mind the talents and character of each individual as well as the needs of society. Some professions are more favorable to intellectual development than others, and a few of them are intellectual endeavors by their very nature. Others make the intellectual life more or less difficult; still others are altogether incompatible with it. Moreover, professional activity leads normally to a retirement age and it is not easy for everyone to adjust to this eventuality.

We offer the following analyses, thoughts, and advice as a psychologist and a psychotherapist. We want at all costs to avoid dogmatism; the solutions here suggested are not the only ones. Individual conditions vary greatly. There are no universal recipes in this book. Each reader will have to make personal appropriation of what we say. The book is intended to incite each reader to ask himself certain questions and answer them in terms of his own situation.

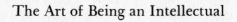

The Art of Being an Intellectual

# 1

# *The Intellectual*

## THE PREDECESSORS

Present-day inellectuals have had illustrious predecessors. In ancient Greece they were called "lovers of wisdom" (*philosophoi*). They gathered about such masters as Socrates, Plato, and Aristotle and were professional students of nature and truth. Those who exercised a profession were usually teachers or tutors in royal households. Later, in Roman times, the art of rhetoric attracted many philosophers. It is well known that Plato recommended intellectuals as the most capable rulers of the city, and as a matter of fact many Greek kings and Roman emperors were lovers of wisdom, the most famous being Solon and Marcus Aurelius. Philosophers were generally held in high respect, the more so perhaps because they were so much better educated than the average citizen. They had their enemies, of course. One of the most celebrated critics of intellectuals was Aristophanes, who wrote them off, often with cruel irony, as hair-splitters. Even Socrates did not escape his wrath. History records that certain unscrupulous

1

pedants capitalized on the philosophers' prestige; they wore
special garb to distinguish themselves from the common run
of men, engaged in empty rhetoric, and were generally re-
ferred to as "sophists." Socrates delighted in unmasking them
and demonstrating their vanity and ignorance to his students.

In Judaism at the time of Christ the local intellectuals
were known as Scribes and Pharisees. According to the Gos-
pel reports they resembled the Greek sophists in their love of
argument and pedantry as well as their interest in the form
rather than the substance of argumentation. But the Jewish
intellectuals were almost exclusively interested in religious
questions, in the interpretation of Scripture and rituals. Only
later during the Diaspora, when they came into contact with
Greek culture, did some of them, like Philo of Alexandria,
begin to show an interest in philosophical reflection and the
natural sciences.

During the Middle Ages the only intellectuals in Western
Europe were the "clerics," mostly priests and monks. Although they were primarily interested in theology, their natural curiosity led them to reflect on all areas of knowledge—
whether philosophy, cosmology, medicine, mathematics, or
physics. They made no significant discoveries in these fields,
but they must be credited with having maintained continuity
with classical culture, thus laying the groundwork for the
intellectual achievements of modern times. It was under their
leadership that the first great European universities, beginning in the twelfth century, were established. Nor were they
entirely responsible for the fact that medieval culture eventually degenerated into a sterile and static scholasticism.

During the Renaissance, from about the middle of the
fourteenth century on, intellectuals were called "humanists."
Although many of these humanists were believers (including

a number of priests and monks), they rebelled against the restrictions which the Church and the scholastics had imposed upon intellectual freedom. In literature and art, as well as in philosophy and the natural sciences, the Renaissance humanists always strove to go back beyond medieval scholasticism to the classical sources. Leonardo da Vinci, Michelangelo, Machiavelli, Copernicus, and Galileo, and later Erasmus and Montaigne are among the most illustrious of Renaissance thinkers. Political leaders like Lorenzo the Magnificent of Florence, following the example of Plato, tried to apply the principles of humanism to politics. Perhaps the influence of intellectuals on social life has never been greater than during the two centuries of the Renaissance. The Reformation, Counter-Reformation, and religious wars which followed put a brutal end to this golden era. It would be two centuries before the intellectuals once again began to make their voice heard and exercise a real influence.

To be sure, Renaissance humanism was not without its faults. Cesare Borgia and other princes who professed humanism gave free reign to their baser instincts; Popes like Alexander VI and Julius II encouraged art and culture but also contributed generously to the moral and religious decadence of the West. The psychological immaturity of the people and their leaders prevented the humanists from fashioning a society according to their ideals. Still, it is altogether remarkable that they were able to do as much as they did.

In the eighteenth century the intellectuals once again became a power, principally in France. In imitation of ancient Greece, they were proud to be known as "philosophers." In the name of "intellectual enlightenment" they launched a bitter struggle against religious "obscurantism," preaching freedom of thought as well as political freedom against an absolute monarchy. It falls outside the scope of this essay to describe in detail the role Voltaire, Diderot, and the other philosophers of the Enlightenment played in bringing about the French Revolution of 1789 and the social and intellectual upheavals which followed. Those who refuse to admit the grave inadequacies and injustices of the old regime exaggerate the influence of philosophers when they make them responsible for the atrocities of the Revolution and all the evils that beset modern man. But, as we shall note with respect to our own age, it is traditional to make intellectuals the scapegoats for all the sins of the world. Already at the time of the Counter-Reformation the humanists were blamed for the moral and religious decadence of the age; but the truth of the matter is that they resisted this decadence, which originated in quite different sources, with all their strength.

## THE INTELLECTUAL TODAY

Beginning with the last decades of the nineteenth century the heirs of the philosophers, clerics, and humanists began to be called "intellectuals." But it is difficult to find agreement upon a definition of the modern intellectual. In certain circles the term is far from a complimentary one. The intellectual, it is said, is a dreamer, a utopian who lives in an ivory tower of abstract ideas. He is by definition incapable of action and understands little of the real problems of life. Since "realism" of this sort is usually politically rightist it follows that the intellectual must be a leftist. When in a speech I spoke incidentally of Charles de Gaulle as an intellectual, my audience was astounded. "But isn't he a rightist?" they objected, thus reflecting the widespread belief, especially in France, that all intellectuals are leftists. At bottom the image which intellectuals enjoy in the eyes of most men today is not substantially different from Aristophanes' caricature of the sophists in *The Clouds*. A recent example of this was the Algerian war. The politicians cruelly satirized those "dear professors" who recommended peace and the right of peoples to manage their own affairs.

Obviously we cannot accept so tendentious a conception of the intellectual. In the strict sense, intellectuals are those who are dedicated to intellectual activity. As in preceding ages, professors and philosophers are most deserving of the title of intellectual. But writers, many artists, as well as scientists who are not content with laboratory research but make syntheses, are likewise intellectuals. And this independently of their political, religious, or philosophical opinions. For, contrary to popular opinion, there are genuine intellectuals who are politically rightist, who are more attached to national and religious traditions than to the mystique of progress. In France, for example, André Malraux and Jacques Soustelle have gone from the militant left to the conservative right without ceasing to be intellectuals.

But we are not concerned only with professional intellectuals. They, after all, are a small minority. Today the notion of intellectual has a much more extended meaning. All those for whom the life of the mind has a preponderant place can be considered intellectuals regardless of their profession. There are many intellectuals among doctors, lawyers, engineers, the clergy, and even among ordinary men and women who have never gone to a university. Contrariwise, there are professors and writers who are in no sense of the word intellectuals because they exercise their profession more or less mechanically and their specifically intellectual preoccupations are minimal. I know two accountants. One of them is a genuine intellectual; the other has no intellectual interests at all. Many workingmen are self-taught intellectuals. They devote their free time to serious reading and discussion. Their limitations stem more from a lack of method than a lack of intelligence. By comparison with such self-taught intellectuals who have a real passion for knowledge there are university professors who are scarcely more than barbarians. Outside of their narrow specialization their reading runs to detective stories and their conversation more to automobiles and racing than to matters intellectual.

Intellectuals are not necessarily more intelligent than other men, for people with limited intelligence can be keenly interested in the life of the mind. On the other hand, some mental ability is necessary to be an intellectual. Since we live in an age where everything is measured and tested, let us say that it would hardly be possible to be an intellectual without a minimal I.Q. of 120.

## THE INTELLECTUAL VOCATION

Some men and women have an authentic intellectual vocation. They realize that whatever other pleasures and successes life might offer them they will not be truly happy unless they dedicate themselves totally to the service of the mind. Unfortunately many such people discover their intellectual vocation too late, after it has become practically impossible for them to change their way of life. It sometimes happens too that external circumstances interfere with this vocation. I have often had occasion to counsel men and women who were psychically sick because they failed to follow their vocation.

Nicholas, forty-one, was a civil servant. He suffered from

anxiety and a sense of failure. His interest in life was at such a low ebb that, in his own words, only laziness prevented him from commiting suicide. In the course of therapy he admitted that early in life he had been greatly attracted by the intellectual life. At an age when other children were still interested in playing he "devoured" book after book on a great variety of subjects. Later he began to visit museums and exhibits. At that time he wanted to be an ethnologist. But that would have taken long years of study and promised little in the way of material security, a factor that was of prime importance to his parents, who were poor and rather limited intellectually. At their insistence, Nicholas entered the civil service. His later career was to all appearances successful. He married, had children and was looked up to his community. But none of this made him happy. He had a gnawing awareness of having failed to follow his true vocation. He bitterly regretted not having known anyone who could have guided and encouraged him to resist his parents' objections.

Of course one cannot become an intellectual by merely wishing it. Nor is it enough to imitate fashionable writers. In one sense, one is born an intellectual, although not in the same way a nobleman is born to the aristocracy. The son of a count is already a count as an infant; but there is no guarantee that the son of an intellectual will be an intellectual. I know a celebrated university professor who was shocked because not one of his six sons got through secondary school or indicated the slightest interest in any form of the intellectual life. On the other hand there are veritable dynasties of intellectuals where son succeeds father for generations. The father's example can be an incentive; but it can also be an obstacle. The son may for one reason or another resent his father and refuse to follow in his footsteps. Or again, the father's prestige may be so great that the son would not dare enter into competition with him.

The qualities required to become an intellectual are gifts of nature transmitted by some unknown process of heredity. But for figures like Camus and Kafka one is hard put to determine the source of the exceptional talent the whole world recognizes in them. I know one famous writer who came from a background that was not only uneducated but moreover tarnished by alcoholism and other vices. His childhood was a painful one, and he was frequently imprisoned. While in prison he began to read and literally educated himself. He began to write at twenty and was already famous by twenty-five. Where does such talent come from? We can scarcely credit heredity in any ordinary sense of the word. This is a problem that neither the psychological nor biological sciences have as yet clarified. The most we can say is that at birth some are musically gifted, others are inclined to philosophy, and still others to scientific research. At most, external conditions can encourage or inhibit the development of these innate tendencies. Neither training nor education suffice to make one an intellectual. On the other hand it frequently happens that the lack of appropriate education prevents someone otherwise qualified from becoming an intellectual. It is highly probable that the writer we mentioned above would never have become aware of his talents if he had not gone to prison. If he had been apprenticed to one of the trades or gone to work in a factory, as most of his friends did, where would he have found time to read?

It is a loss for both the individuals themselves and for society at large that those who feel drawn to an intellectual vocation cannot realize it. It is likely that Nicholas, whose case we outlined earlier, would have become a great ethnologist if family opposition had not interfered. But others overcome all obstacles. Thus one of the most original of modern French philosophers began life as a rural postman. But he eventually acquired the necessary degrees and became a professor at the Sorbonne. A current member of the French Academy began his career in a shoe factory. Neither neuroses nor various illnesses prevented Blaise Pascal from achieving extraordinary intellectual eminence. The same could be said for Toulouse-Lautrec, Verlaine, Nietzsche, and Kafka. Of course we are discussing genuises here, and they can scarcely serve as models for "ordinary" intellectuals. But many of the latter succeed precisely because of the obstacles they have had to overcome.

An intellectual vocation can be scientific as well as literary. But it is not enough to be a great physician, a good philologist, or a brilliant jurist to merit the title of intellectual. The true intellectual is one who goes far beyond the limits of his specialty. He must aspire to be a worthy successor of the "clerics" and "humanists" of former times. I recall attending a banquet with a famous microbiologist and a no less famous musicologist. In the course of the meal they had very little to say to one another. This was because the microbiologist could only talk about a certain kind of tropical flea and the musicologist was equally specialized. It is clear that neither gentleman was an intellectual in the proper sense of that word. Yet by broadening the field of their interests both could have been intellectuals without in any way compromising their specialty. A well-known French psychiatrist, who has made original contributions in his field, is also an accomplished man of letters and the author of a number of books that are authoritative in their own right. Einstein's passion for music and keen interest in problems of the human community are well known. But this scarcely prevented him from being a highly skilled and effective scientist.

It is neither necessary nor possible that all intellectuals be as universal as, say, Leonardo da Vinci or Blaise Pascal. Here we have to do with geniuses. But all must achieve a minimum of universality, otherwise their own human fulfillment will suffer as well as science itself. Unfortunately such fulfillment is not encouraged by the narrow specialization that one generally finds in the United States and Soviet Russia and which is beginning to infiltrate other countries as well. In the strict sense of the word we no longer have any *universities* but only *faculties* that are rigidly separated from one another. We will have occasion to say more on this theme later on. For the moment let us emphasize that this situation constitutes a serious threat to the intellectual future of mankind. If the danger cannot be offset, in a few decades intellectuals will be an extinct breed. Genius will continue to exist but in a very small minority. Let us hope that this extreme will never eventuate, for it would cause great harm to the individuals themselves and to the human community in general.

## THE INTELLIGENTSIA

In former times the "clerics" constituted a well-defined social class with special privileges and social responsibilities. Modern intellectuals constitute neither a class nor a caste; they are mere individuals. At most they form a "school" because they profess some common principle or acknowledge the same master. As a result of the rampant individualism of the past few centuries intellectuals are far less conscious of their social obligations; in devoting themselves to science or philosophy, art or literature they are solely concerned with their own fulfillment, even if this must be achieved to the detriment of the collectivity.

An exception is the Russia of the last quarter of the nineteenth century. The intellectuals there, although few in number, were keenly aware of their responsibilities and duties to the people. Nourished by the philosophy of the French Enlightenment and German romanticism, they considered it their double duty to fight against the tyranny of Tsarist absolutism and educate the people. Young noblemen with university educations became country schoolteachers and at the same time plotted against the tsars and their ministers. The Church was completely under the sway of the ruling oligarchy and seemed intent upon keeping the people in ignorance. Consequently the Russian intellectuals took up the gauntlet against the clerical establishment and, by implication, against religion. Thus was born the *intelligentsia,* a collective designation for committed intellectuals.

Of course, not all Russian intellectuals were progressive. Some served either the state or the Church and denied that education could make the people happier. But they were not part of the intelligentsia.

Although it originated in Russia, the term *intelligentsia* is today found, more or less happily, in all the languages of the world. This is because a large number of intellectuals, especially in the West, are getting beyond the individualism of the past centuries and becoming conscious of their social responsibilities, of their role as *intellectuals* in the present moment of history. The intelligentsia in the West is less homogeneous than the original Russian intelligentsia. We speak of a liberal, Catholic or even Communist intelligentsia. But they all have certain features in common. They share a certain fidelity to the old humanist tradition. On the list of those who regularly sign petitions against capital punishment, torture, and the oppression of underdeveloped nations are usually found men of both the right and the left, both believers and unbelievers. It is to their credit that most members of the intelligentsia are against injustice and oppression in whatever form. Thus intellectuals as a whole have not renounced the universality of their tradition. Only Communist intellectuals are restricted by party allegiance in this respect. But even in this case we should note that many of them sided with the Hungarian and Polish insurgents in 1956. Some left the party and others were exiled, while most of the non-intellectuals apparently had little difficulty adapting to the current party line.

That intellectuals are renouncing their narcissism and becoming conscious of their social responsibilities is obviously a cause for rejoicing. But they must guard against excesses of zeal. In France, for example, it is always the same professors, writers, and journalists who sign all petitions in favor of noble causes or what strikes them as such. This results in a lack of discrimination, for they often don't take the trouble to inform themselves of the facts. This in turn leads to a loss of prestige for the intelligentsia in the public eye. It would be easy enough for the adversaries of the causes they defend to capitalize on their mistakes and cripple their legitimate social mission.

# 2

# *A Letter to*
# *a Young Intellectual*

I shall be only too happy, Daniel, if I can be of any assistance in helping you realize your ambition to become an intellectual. Such an ambition is neither ridiculous nor illegitimate. Christ himself said that the violent shall conquer the kingdom of heaven. We may fittingly translate "violent" as "ambitious." In any case a young man without ambition is not likely to go far. Only a false humility could condemn ambition. The saints had plenty of ambition, for the glory of God if not for themselves. Your ambition, Daniel, to achieve something worthwhile in the intellectual domain is far nobler than that of so many of your friends to make as much money as they can with the least expenditure of effort.

Our ambitions of course must be determined by our ability, otherwise we invite failure and discouragement. I knew you when you were a mere seven or eight years old and already I discerned a future intellectual. You asked me and

13

other friends of the family probing questions far beyond your years. You were interested in things and listened attentively to our various conversations on literature, art, philosophy, theology, and politics. Naturally you only understood bits and snatches; but you remembered everything. And how you read! So much so that at times your parents became concerned. Nothing could give you greater pleasure than receiving books as presents. Over the years your library grew both quantitatively and qualitatively. You began with children's books and then graduated to travelogues, then history and literature, and, finally, to science and philosophy. To all appearances you have an intellectual vocation and also the necessary talents to realize it. Soon you will have to choose your future profession and the university studies that will prepare you for it.

I hope that my advice will be of some profit to you and to other young men like you.

## READING

There is no point in insisting on the fact that only those who like to read have an chance of becoming authentic intellectuals. I know there are writers and scientists who think more than they read. But they are a minority and more or less pathological at that. I have met intellectuals who thought they had invented original scientific theories or launched absolutely unprecedented social reforms capable of changing the world. But when I read them it was painfully obvious that what they had to say had long been known and in many cases had become old-fashioned. The greatest thinkers in history never pretended to create out of nothing. They viewed their contributions as links in the great chain of human thought and considered themselves part of a humanity that is one and indivisible in space and time. Those who withdraw from the human community by cutting the bonds that link the present with the past and each individual thinker with others very likely have schizoid tendencies; at any rate, their chances of authentic achievements are rare.

I am of the opinion that the young intellectual should read broadly: novels of all kinds, biographies, history and geography, popular science and, later on, philosophical and theological works. A certain eclecticism seems desirable in the first stages of intellectual development. Almost all genuine intellectuals with whom I have had the opportunity to discuss this question have told me that they read widely and derived much profit from so acting. The only criterion of selection, especially for literary works, should be their artistic value. I am aware, of course, that many parents and educators are concerned about the bad influence that certain books might have on the immature. I think most of their fears are exaggerated. I have not encountered a single instance where books by such authors as Gide and Arthur Miller have had a pernicious influence on serious young readers; many were not even aware of the immoral content of such books. The same is not true of those who read little and without any great intellectual interest. These do not in fact enjoy reading and seek in books something other than the discovery of unknown worlds. But for young people with serious intellectual dispositions reading worthwhile books, even if they leave something to be desired from the moral point of view, not only contributes to their intellectual formation and increases their knowledge but also refines their sensibility and matures their emotional character. Educators too often forget that, both emotionally and intellectually, nature has only given us a

potential which must be actualized. And the process of identi-
fication which reading fosters is one of the best ways of actu-
alizing our innate dispositions. Gradually, after a succession
of identifications, our own intelligence and sensibility begin
to take form. From this point of view a limited reading program is much more likely to have harmful effects because in
that case the young reader only identifies with one model and
consequently bases his intellectual and emotional behavior
on that image which may not be suited to his personality at
all.

Eventually the young intellectual will become more selective in his reading. Some will be more interested in historical
works; others will gravitate towards philosophy or ethnology;
still others will be inclined to novels and literary criticism.
The last mentioned will usually try their hand at writing,
even though they may never become professional writers. A
young intellectual with scientific interests should never completely give up reading literary and philosophical works. The
contempt many young scientists have for literature and especially philosophy is a serious weakness. Only spiritual famili-
arity with the great thinkers can enable the scientist to become a genuine scholar, a man capable of transcending the
necessarily narrow limits—and they are becoming even nar-
rower as science progresses—of his specialty to achieve a syn-
thetic vision. The great scientific minds of our times—Albert
Einstein, Bertrand Russell, Pierre Teilhard de Chardin, Jean
Rostand, and many others—were informed about philosophy
and general culture and in some cases were philosophers in
their own right.

Curiosity, that thirst to know and to learn, will impel the
young intellectual to read widely. And he should at all costs
be encouraged to do so. The cultural treasures of mankind

are immense, and only by familiarizing ourselves with them can we become aware of their extraordinary richness. The man of little education is easily persuaded that he knows everything while the intellectual is aware that he knows very little. But he should have favorite books and authors which he rereads frequently. When you are a little older, Daniel, do not feel that it would be a waste of time to reread works which you found particularly interesting and stimulating when you first read them. At thirty we find much more in a book than we did at twenty; the older we get the more benefit we derive from reading. For example, I recently reread a book by Bergson which had a decisive influence on my intellectual orientation when I was eighteen years old. I was surprised to discover so much in it that I had missed when I first read it, while what first impressed me seemed quite uninteresting. I have had the same experience with many other books I was impressed with when I was young. The day will come, Daniel, when you will learn more from rereading the great masters than from reading the most recently published books. But for the moment it is better to read widely.

## INITIATION INTO
## INTELLECTUAL WORK

A simple criterion for reading is that it profit us in some way. Even books we completely forget can be of some profit. The unconscious retains the substance and assimilates it to our general intellectual outlook. Many of our ideas, even those we take to be most original and personal, derive from books we no longer remember. These books furnished the seed of our ideas; it then germinated and developed according to the structures of our individual psyche; the resultant ideas can, consequently, rightly be considered our own. But in many cases it is desirable for the conscious memory to retain what we learn from reading. But however good our memories be, they are far from infallible. Thus such memory aids as note-taking are highly recommended.

You, Daniel, and other young intellectuals who have not yet settled on a career, would be well advised to take copious notes on all that you read. You should have a notebook for each genre of book: historical, philosophical, scientific, etc. Nor should novels be neglected, for we often find ideas and forms of expression in them that should be remembered. As soon as you begin a book write the title, author, and publisher at the beginning of your notebook. Don't hesitate to pause in the middle of even the most engrossing passages to note a given phrase that particularly struck you, or a thought inspired by your reading. After you have finished the book write a brief summary and express your own judgment on it. Even if you never use these notes, having taken them is nonetheless a profitable exercise. They will help you clarify and criticize your own reaction, which might otherwise remain too vague.

Later, when you have chosen your specialty, you will have to adopt a filing system. This will enable you to classify your notes in a more organized way (according to author or subject) for ready reference. But you should continue the practice of taking notes; this will be particularly helpful with respect to books outside of your field. For I sincerely hope you will continue to be interested in aspects of the intellectual life other than your specialty.

You should always carry a special notebook on your person to record those thoughts that come to us spontaneously—

whether while traveling, relaxing, or walking in the park. Such thoughts can be of great help to you in your work. Unfortunately, if not jotted down when they come to us they are lost forever. One of my friends is never separated from his notepad and luminous pencil. When traveling at night or awakening from sleep he often has occasion to note those sudden inspirations that come unsolicited and often prove useful to him in his professional life.

## AUDIO·VISUAL CULTURE

When I was young books were still the principal source of education. What we knew about the outside world and the ideas that inspired men and society we learned from reading. Don't be too surprised then, Daniel, if your parents and teachers sometimes seem too "bookish." It is difficult for them not to be.

Your generation learns a good deal from movies, radio, and television. Teen-agers of former times had to exercise their imagination to form a more or less adequate idea of the love they read about in novels; today even children witness in movies long, passionate kisses and frequently detailed bedroom scenes. The realities of love hold no secrets for them. Such precocious initiation obviously presents certain dangers for the psychic and moral health of young people, and parents should not let children see films they are not mature enough to digest. Nonetheless it remains true that the knowledge we acquire through movies and television is much more concrete than what we learn through reading. Foreign peoples and countries, exotic animals, adventure and exploration, the beauty of the desert, the depths of the sea and the stratosphere are grasped with infinitely greater truth by the televiewer than the reader. As such audio-visual culture is not absolutely new. It is somewhat comparable to what our ancestors learned, in the Middle Ages for example, by contemplating art works in the cathedrals or attending mystery plays. But the content of today's visual media is very different from medieval imagery. The culture of the West became exclusively bookish only in recent centuries as a result of our interest in general education.

Unfortunately these new means of education are not free from dangers. In the first place, we must note the almost irresistible fascination that the flow of images has for most people, especially the young. Some people are analogously fascinated by reading detective or adventure stories. But the fascination produced by images on the screen is much greater and makes a much more indelible impression on the psyche. The difference here is less the narrative than the mechanical sequence of images. It is common enough to observe young children absorbed in a film even though its meaning escapes them entirely. A similar phenomenon obtains for television, regardless of the program content. The same is true for many adults. I know people who go to two or three movies on their day off. Others watch television all day or let the radio play for hours on end. And we all realize that since the advent of television conversation has become a lost art. Even the family dinner is no excuse to turn the television set off.

Another danger resulting from the audio-visual media is that many young people have lost all interest in reading. While what we learn from imagery is much more concrete, it is at the same time more superficial than knowledge acquired by reading. This was brought home to me by a little experiment I recently conducted. I interrogated two groups of teen-agers. One had read Tolstoy's *War and Peace*. The other had only seen the movie based on that novel. The first exhibited a much more profound comprehension both of the psychological implications and historical background of the novel. I repeated the experiment apropos of Stendhal's *The Red and the Black* and several other novels that had been made into movies. The result was always the same. The triumph of the screen over the book has brought about a perceptible narrowing of cultural awareness as well as a dangerous reduction of psychological awareness.

Have no fear, Daniel, that I am among those who condemn what is new in the name of the pretended superiority of traditional values. I have no intention of doing battle against the new media; that would be like Don Quixote fighting the windmills. All efforts to return to some golden age of the past are utopian. One day the automobile may be replaced by the helicopter; but we may be sure there will be no return to the days of the stagecoach. Whatever the imperfections of industrial society there can be no return to the age of the artisan.

To return to our subject, I am not recommending *resignation* to the audio-visual media as an inevitable evil; quite the contrary, I have no hesitation in praising them as instruments of authentic progress. I have already mentioned some of their advantages. Nor let us forget that it is because of television that those who live in villages and other remote places are able to transcend their isolation and communicate with the whole world. What goes on in Africa or Asia concerns such people today, whereas their fathers scarcely knew what was going on in the next town. However, the new media must be used intelligently.

There is an important difference, Daniel, between a desire "to go to the movies" and the desire to see a given film. In the first case, one seeks escape from boredom, to flee from the real in life, while in the second case one seeks to satisfy a legitimate artistic or scientific curiosity. It is quite all right to go to the movies for amusement but here again one must be selective. Too much time spent in dimly lit rooms can have harmful effects on our psychological equilibrium. Almost all psychologists are agreed that the less children under fourteen go to the movies the better off they are.

It is more difficult to lay down rules for television. But a good rule of thumb is to turn the set on only when there is a program we are genuinely interested in seeing. And what is true for the cinema also holds for television: children should be permitted to watch only what they are capable of understanding. At all costs television should not be allowed to interfere with that unique family gathering which is the evening meal. To resist the temptation to watch programs of little or no worth, I have advised many families to install the television set elsewhere than in the living room. In this way one is more likely to exercise discrimination.

It is especially important to understand that the audiovisual media are not a substitute for reading but rather a complement. You should reserve a certain period of time each day, Daniel, for reading. And should you become a father and a teacher, see to it that you inculcate a love of reading in your charges. Love of reading is far from a backward trait; completed by other sources of information it will in the future contribute much more effectively than in the past to the progress of humanity and individuals.

## THE WRITER'S WORK

One day you may write a book or become a professional writer. Thus some advice along these lines might be in order.

The first requisite for writing a good book is obviously to

have something to say, to communicate to others. I wrote my
first book when I was fifteen; but that was clearly a prema-
ture effort. My experience of life and men was necessarily too
limited and, furthermore, I was too close to what experience
I did have. It later became clear to me that my first novel was
primarily a digest of the different books I had read. I don't
mean that young people shouldn't be encouraged to write;
but it should be considered more an exercise, an apprentice-
ship, and not intended for publication. Our early efforts with
the pen can be circulated among our friends and perhaps
submitted to a professional writer for criticism. A well-known
writer has said: "Good literature is what has germinated and
flowered within us over a period of fifteen or twenty years. So
much the worse for child prodigies!" Child prodigies do come
along now and again but they are rare. Just how long a book
should mature is a relative matter. Some may take fifteen or
twenty years. Others mature much more quickly, depending
on the character of the writer. Some writers are late bloomers,
while others are guided by sudden inspirations. Many ideas
have to be caught on the wing, as it were; otherwise, far from
germinating and flowering, they will dry up altogether.

How a book is to be written depends on the temperament
of each writer. A methodical writer will begin with a detailed
outline and follow it through to the end. Such writers have
usually done a good deal of research, even if they are writing
novels. Another class of writer, and I should include myself
here, follow a more intuitive course and let the book's pattern
emerge progressively as they write it. They start with a sudden inspiration, and only after they have worked it out are
they able to discern an order and structure. My own ideas for
books have always come from dialogue with others. I live
with an idea for weeks, months, or even years; I organize my

thinking and reading in terms of it and jot down in a note-book whatever is even remotely connected with the idea. Then one day the pattern of what I want to do crystallizes and I begin the actual writing. During the period of gestation I make tentative chapter headings, but the table of contents only becomes definite as the work progresses. Once the period of gestation is over, I write quickly. I never know what to answer when I am asked how long it took me to write a given book. In the strict sense of "writing" perhaps two or three months; but the preparatory period may have lasted for years. Once the rough draft is completed I begin the second version on a typewriter. Frequently enough this is radically different from the first. Because I rework my material so extensively, it is impossible to dictate; consequently I have to do my own typing. Of course, Daniel, there is no reason why you should follow my example. I merely cite it to make it easier for you to determine your own procedure.

Some authors labor over their manuscripts indefinitely; they even make important corrections on the proof pages. One celebrated theologian of my acquaintance is never satisfied enough with his manuscript to authorize publication. His editors have to force his hand and forbid further corrections. This kind of intellectual perfectionism is analogous to moral scrupulosity and is equally neurotic. Personally, I do little more than correct typographical errors on the final version. Not that I think my work is perfect. But perfection is not easily achieved, and I console myself with the thought that I can develop my ideas in a later work. This method, of course, won't suit everyone. The individual writer has to work out the most effective method for him. But the important thing, as I said before, is for the writer to have something to say, to feel he has a message to communicate.

In literary writing, however, the style is as important as the content, sometimes more so. There are masterpieces whose intellectual content is very slight, whose value is almost exclusively aesthetic. Their authors are primarily artists, although they may be at the same time authentic intellectuals. Furthermore, even in a scholarly work whose value resides primarily in its content, form has its importance. Some scientific and philosophical books deal with very important subjects, but they are so badly written that the reader can scarcely understand them. There are others like the philosophical writings of Bergson, Lavelle, and Guardini and the scientific works of Jean Rostand and Leprince-Ringuet that are characterized as much by their literary grace as by originality of content. I have often heard outstanding scientists jealously denigrate their colleagues' success with the public and judge their work inferior for this reason. But the superiority of the successful man very probably derives from his capacity to communicate in an intelligible fashion; and that is a very real superiority.

There are no universal rules for good style. It is determined both by the writer's temperament and the subject matter being treated. But we may state unequivocally that no style can be called good unless it is clear. Obscurity is not a necessary concomitant of difficult themes. Scientists have written on very profound matters in a style that any educated person could read without great difficulty. There is an element of snobbism in disdainfully regarding them as "popularizers" because they communicate the fruit of their personal research and thought. Thus the best style is, in my opinion, the one that makes reading pleasurable, and I am convinced that even the most profound and serious works can be enjoyable reading for educated people. Moreover, our age is not fond of fanciful writing. Good style must be simple and direct, although imagery and metaphors have their place.

Assiduous reading of good books seems to me the only effective means of developing a good style. There is no question here of slavishly imitating an author whose style we admire. But good stylists help us immeasurably in forming our own style, although their influence is often largely unconscious. We might say that we have acquired a satisfactory individual style when we no longer consciously imitate another, when it flows spontaneously from our pen, although there will always be a place for further improvement. It is also good to let two or three weeks pass before we reread what we have written. This will permit us a certain necessary objectivity in passing judgment upon it.

Course work and lectures are also of great value. While books may seem more stylistic than lectures by professors or public figures, the latter have the advantage of bringing you into contact with people who are worthy of your admiration. Too, we can learn a good deal from the collective reactions of an audience. Even attendance at political rallies is instructive in this respect. Discussion groups have a similar value because they stimulate dialogue and the confrontation of ideas. They will provide you with an opportunity to discipline your own thinking and express your ideas in terms of others.

Should you become a professor, writer, lawyer, or journalist try always to remember that you will write and speak for others and not for yourself. It is difficult for an ivory-tower intellectual to be creative, and he is not likely to have any real influence on his contemporaries. Publishers receive all kinds of manuscripts every day; they are often quite original and have a certain objective value; but they are vitiated by the fact that the authors visibly wrote only for themselves,

and consequently they have little chance of acquiring a reading public. It is vain to show contempt, as some do, for the
public and write solely for oneself or a few close friends.
They should not be surprised when publishers return their
efforts with a polite rejection slip. If you should one day de-
cide to publish a book, always bear in mind your readers.
And if you are preparing a course or a public lecture always
strive to maintain mental communication with your audience. To be sure, every intellectual is normally and above all
a servant of the truth. But one cannot effectively serve truth
merely by proclaiming it. It must be presented in an attrac-
tive manner; the audience must be convinced. The word
"propaganda" has of late been devalued by many abuses; yet
it pertains to the intellectual vocation to propagate the
truth.

## LEARNING HOW TO JUDGE

Wide reading and knowledge of many things does not
make an intellectual. One must judge what has been learned,
seen, and understood. This implies a criterion of judgment.
For works of art like music, painting, sculpture, the dance,
and poetry this criterion is primarily of the aesthetic order,
although other factors such as ethical considerations sometimes must play an equally important role. Just because a
work of art is beautiful is not a sufficient reason for admiring
it unreservedly. A strip tease can be performed very aestheti-
cally but it does not follow that I would recommend that you
frequent such performances. On the other hand, it is also
true that good intentions do not guarantee the validity of a
work of art. Pious art such as that found in the Saint Sulpice
area of Paris is no doubt inspired by good intentions; but,

even from the point of view of the religion which it pretends to serve, it does more harm than good.

When it is a question of judging human acts, of taking a position on war and peace, racial equality, politics, or religion, it is evident that an aesthetic criterion has a far more limited function. We must have some clear ideas about good and evil. The Luciferian type of intellectual is in reality very dangerous for the human community; he can become destructive, even criminal. Those who have been inspired by Nietzsche's *Zarathustra* or Wagner's *Twilight of the Gods* and believe that it is enough to do something great to become supermen have succeeded only in strewing history with collective and individual catastrophes.

Intellectuals are frequently accused of judging events in a purely abstract way. They adhere too rigidly to principles, so the accusation runs, without taking the concrete realities sufficiently into account. This charge is not always justified. Oftentimes anti-intellectual men of action have too restricted a conception of what reality is. The intellectual naturally adopts a wider perspective. Thus with regard to the colonial wars of recent decades, it is by no means a proven fact that the intellectuals who argued for the freedom of colonial peoples were less "realistic" than those who, ignoring historical evolution, tried to maintain the old order of things. On the other hand, the accusation that intellectuals are too abstract and unrealistic is sometimes well founded. This is most frequently because their formation has been too exclusively bookish. They were taught to judge reality in terms of general principles and theories. Consequently they are ill at ease with contingent situations and the emotional motives of human actions. An intelligentsia that is too removed from the people will be ineffective and unfaithful to its vocation.

## THE CHOICE OF TEACHERS

You have told me, Daniel, of the contempt which many of your friends have for those who might have some influence on them. Because they want to be totally themselves and become strong individuals, they refuse to admire anyone and adopt an attitude of skeptical indifference towards their teachers. I beg you not to imitate them. Those who put on airs and affirm that they are self-sufficient and need no leaders are likely to be covering up a weakness. Moreover, they are mistaken if they think they are free of all influences. The worst kind of influence works on our subconscious because it is generally exercised by those whom consciously we absolutely refuse to imitate. The man of really strong character has a well-structured self and knows full well that no human being is self-sufficient, that each of us has need of others to become ourselves. A man with self-confidence, far from rejecting the influence of others, will freely choose the teacher whom he thinks most capable of helping him become himself. Not many have tried to pursue an ideal by themselves. Almost always they discover themselves through another. The greatest minds readily admit that at a given moment in their lives, generally in their youth, they met a teacher who inspired them to become what they are.

There are, of course, enslaving influences. They derive not so much from any objective value in those who wield them as from their ability to mesmerize the crowds. One thinks of Hitler, Stalin, and Mussolini. When we recall the veritable collective hysteria that recently overcame one of the most educated countries in history during the Nazi regime, we can understand why some are suspicious of all authority. They fear they might be led to do things they have no desire to do.

Even intellectual prestige can be a dangerous thing. Sartre, who in the name of "existentialism" rejected all the values of civilization and all absolutes, had a great influence on young people after World War II. And how many crimes have been committed in the name of Nietzsche's philosophy! I do not mean to imply that Sartre would have recognized his authentic disciples in the misled groups that frequented the cafés of Paris or that Nietzsche would have approved of the crimes against human dignity committed in his name. Nonetheless, objectively speaking, the Sartrian and Nietzschean influence has caused much harm.

But admitting that some influences can be harmful and rejecting all influence are two different matters. Some influences can be liberating and elevating. And this is what we are concerned with. There is no danger that such influence will prevent you from becoming yourself. The true teacher, and I hope you become one, does not want his disciple to abdicate his own personality and become a banal echo of himself. He requires no servile imitation. You will discover your real self under his influence. It is not a question of wanting to become like your teacher but of becoming as much yourself as he is himself. Bergson once told me that he considered his best students not those who continually proclaimed what Bergson had said, thus making of "Bergsonism" a dull repetition of the master's words, but those who sought the truth with the same love and fidelity as he did, even though their quest should lead them to a radically different position.

Since you are a young intellectual, you are naturally most sensitive to intellectual influences. But do not be a student of one master. Just as the man of one book easily becomes sectarian, so too there is a similar danger in the man of one master. He becomes fanatical, loses his critical sense and takes positions on subjective rather than objective grounds. Follow your mentor with affection and appreciation but without fanaticism. Nor is there any reason why you cannot have more than one mentor, or change mentors if you should so desire. Your teacher at eighteen will not likely be of much help to you when you are twenty-five. There is no doubt that one of the great blessings for a young intellectual is to meet a master whom he can approach, who takes a personal interest in him and is willing to counsel and guide him. Such a master could be a great man long dead whose influence is perpetuated through his works.

Intellectual competence is not the only criterion for choosing a mentor; he should also have moral and spiritual qualities. If men like Bergson, Einstein, and Lord Russell, for example, were great intellectual leaders it was as much because of their qualities *as men* as because of the eminent value of their work. Aspire, Daniel, to become not merely a great intellectual but a great man. The two do not necessarily go hand in hand; but neither are they mutually exclusive.

# 3

# *To Each His Own*

As we have said, the profession does not make an intellectual. There are authentic intellectuals among manual laborers and, conversely, there are reputed intellectuals who in no sense of the word deserve the appellation, so far are they from according primacy to the things of the mind. They simply had the opportunity to pursue higher studies and as a result became university professors or editors. But our psychological makeup is such that we can only realize ourselves as individuals and best serve society if our professional activity is in harmony with our emotional structure. Some professions are so at variance with our real talents and tastes that we would condemn ourselves to sterility and unhappiness if we engaged in them. Psychologists are familiar with the phenomenon of highly educated men and women who have lost all interest in life. Often enough the cause of their sense of failure and boredom turns out to be that they are maladjusted professionally. Formerly, when the rhythm of life was slower, one could find fulfillment outside of professional activity. But today things are different. Our personal fulfillment is generally bound up with our profession.

Let us take the case of George. At the age of eighteen he was sent by his parents to specialize in commerce—not because this was what he wanted but because he came from a long line of important businessmen. When he graduated he entered the family business and became president at the age of thirty after his father died. Ten years later his personal physician advised him to see a psychotherapist. He suffered from depression and a strong sense of failure, both on the professional and marital level (for his marriage had been contracted primarily on social and family grounds). He had little self-confidence and was afraid to make decisions or give orders to his staff. He had been suffering from this depression for some five years at regular intervals. Neurological treatment had no effect. Yet he had an I.Q. of 132. In the course of treatment it became clear that George was unhappy in his profession; had it not been for family pressure he would have gravitated toward a literary career. He could only be completely cured by changing professions. But this is unfortunately rarely possible for someone over forty with heavy family and social responsibilities.

Preparation for an intellectual profession generally requires long years of study. It is important, then, to make an early choice—not later than the end of secondary studies. But the difficulty here is that young people seventeen or eighteen years old are not usually adequately aware of their tastes and talents. They are also difficult to counsel. Parents are more often than not guided by their own frustrated interests than by the real interests of their children. This is another syndrome very familiar to psychologists.

# CHARACTEROLOGICAL INDICATIONS

The great progress realized in the psychological sciences over the past quarter of this century can be of great help in choosing a profession; at least they can prevent the choice of a career that is radically opposed to one's psychological needs. Thus those with an I.Q. of less than 120 should be discouraged from going on for higher studies. But this is not a sufficient criterion. It seems to me that the evidence furnished by characterology must also be taken into consideration. Even a superficial knowledge of George's character would have made it clear that he should have been discouraged from any profession requiring business sense and the ability to give orders.

The three constitutive properties of character are the emotions, action, and memory. Those with quick memories are called "primary," while those with slow memories are "secondary." The three constitutive properties give rise to eight character types: emotive-inactive-primary (nervous); emotive-inactive-secondary (sentimental); emotive-active-primary (choleric); emotive-active-secondary (passionate); non-emotive-active-primary (sanguine); non-emotive-active-secondary (phlegmatic); non-emotive-inactive-primary (amorphous); non-emotive-inactive-secondary (apathetic). It is well to bear in mind that pure types do not exist; we are talking here of dominant characteristics. Moreover, the amorphous and apathetic are not intelligent enough to become intellectuals, so there is no need to talk about them here.

The nervous type lives in the moment, a victim of transitory impulses and impressions. Of uneven temperament, he fluctuates from enthusiasm to discouragement and is not suited to those professions that demand perseverance. Many of the great artists belonged to this category: Baudelaire, Chateaubriand, Byron, Verlaine, A. de Musset, D'Annunzio, Van Gogh, Gauguin, and numerous others.

The sentimental type is sensitive and often suffers because of life's reversals. Because he is a "secondary" he resists the temptation to react and thus represses his emotions. He is meditative, introverted, scrupulous, timid, objective, often indecisive and individualistic, sometimes inclined to misanthropy. He is ambitious but lacks the will power to translate his dreams into reality. Professions that call for social presence are not for him. Because of his taste for things past he is likely to be interested in history, archeology, scientific research, or philosophical reflection. Calvin, Kierkegaard, Berdyaev, Rousseau, Robespierre and Lucretius are some examples of this type.

The choleric in many ways resembles the type categorized as sanguine by the old psychology. He is impulsive and excitable (like the nervous temperament) but since he is active, he is given to commitment. He is a gifted speaker, adapts well to places and circumstances, and is very vivacious. He is ardent and sociable, hopeful of the future but little inclined to contemplation. He rarely sins by default, quite often by excess. On the whole, this type succeeds best in life. They are made for action and initiative rather than laborious research. They are much more interested in the present than the past. Thus they are not likely to find fulfillment as librarians, historians, administrators, or contemplative monks. But they are capable of becoming excellent journalists, politicians, psychotherapists, preachers, public relations officers, and can work in other professions that deal with people more than with things. This kind of character is often encountered among the more gifted Mediterranean peoples. Peguy, Dante, Balzac, Jaurès, Victor Hugo, and Dickens were choleric personalities.

The passionate person is also an active-emotive type and shares most of the qualities of the preceding category, but because he is secondary he is less impulsive and more reflective. He is also stricter, more authoritarian and calculating—traits that give him greater strength. He is not afraid of obstacles, has a great capacity for work and a good deal of continuity in his ideas. He is attracted by the past, is inclined to be conservative and traditionalist, with little sympathy for social transformation. He has a taste for greatness. On the religious plane he is more ascetic than mystical, more moralistic than generous. While the choleric make excellent politicians, the passionate have the qualifications to become statesmen, administrators, business entrepreneurs, researchers, and philosophers. They are at home in professions which demand more stability than brilliance, although they can be quite brilliant in their own right. Men of passionate temperament can be tormented (Beethoven, Tolstoy, St. Augustine, Pascal); meditative (Michelangelo, Molière); imperious (Foch, Richelieu, Napoleon, Lenin); stern (Joseph de Maistre); circumspect (Goethe); industrious (Flaubert, Zola); and methodical (Thomas Aquinas, Raymond Poincaré, Descartes).

The sanguine man is distinguished by his practical sense. Non-emotive, he can readily turn his activity and social relations to utilitarian ends. He is ambitious with respect to short-range projects and thus does not often accomplish great things. With a good sense of observation and much presence of mind, he is more partial to financial success than glory. In politics he is an opportunist. He is clever rather than intelligent, and lacks originality and depth. He is not very religious because his empirical mentality sees nothing practical in religion. He has little interest in women and marries more for reasons of convenience than love. Secretive and calculating, he is likely to be successful in diplomacy and business. Talleyrand, Voltaire, Mazarin, Metternich, Machiavelli, and Anatole France are some examples of sanguine personalities.

The phlegmatic is characterized by perseverance, ponderousness, sobriety, simplicity, objectivity, coldness, and lack of enthusiasm. He is a man of order, skeptical, formal, mildly religious. He has a sense of humor and often likes animals more than people. All forms of business, strategy, conservative politics, mathematics, and science offer the phlegmatic the best opportunity for self-realization. This type of personality is often found among the English and Germans. Kant, Montaigne, d'Alembert, Joffre, Renan, Taine, and Washington were in varying degrees phlegmatics.

## TYPOLOGY

Characterological indications should be complemented by the discoveries of depth psychology. And the psychologist, especially if he is a psychotherapist as well, knows even better than the characterologist that pure types are rarely encountered in real life. But a diagnosis of a person's principal character traits enables us to understand and guide him better.

Carl Jung divides people into introverts and extroverts. The introvert stresses the self and subjectivity while the extrovert subordinates the subject to the object. In other words, an extrovert normally lets his activity and decisions be guided by exterior events rather than his own ideas or personal theories. He thinks, feels, acts, and lives in immediate accord with the demands of objective conditions. He may of course have his own opinions and ideas; but they do not predominate. When there is a conflict between his personal convictions and external imperatives he will obey the latter. Normally the extrovert is more inclined to observe and study the world than to introspection. He has a keen interest in both people and things. This does not mean that he is superficial. He easily assumes many roles but does not necessarily identify with any one of them. But generally professional and social success is more important to him than his interior life or even his health. If he is a philosopher or scientist, he is more interested in practical rather than theoretical problems. Thus he makes a mediocre metaphysician but an excellent psychologist, sociologist, or moralist.

The introvert lives in a subjective world even when he is dealing with objects, other people, or the external world. He is most at home in the world of ideas. He almost always acts in terms of his personal needs rather than the real world. He is capable of great dedication to others, but he must first of all identify with their cause. He forges his theories and determines his outlook in response to his own problems and only by extension can he apply them to others, for he basically believes that others are not very different from himself. If he is a philosopher, metaphysics and logic will attract him. If he is a professor or a clergyman, he will be primarily interested in his personal ideas and theories and only secondarily concerned with their impact on his students or congregation. He is more interested in depth than breadth. He could make a first-rate researcher, especially if he resists the temptation to be doctrinaire and dogmatic.

Introversion and extroversion are innate structural dispositions of the psyche. Under the dominion of neurotic conflicts they can become too rigid and exclusive, thus diminishing the social effectiveness and personal happiness of their subjects. While it is impossible to change an introvert into an extrovert and vice versa, psychotherapy can remedy neurotic excesses in both temperaments. Extroverts are more numerous in the category characterologists call "primary" and introverts tend to be "secondary," but there are many secondary extroverts and primary introverts.

In some people character traits are clearly defined. They can be easily directed to a compatible profession. But in most cases we are confronted with ambiguous, even contradictory, personalities. Apparent extroversion might be nothing more than unconscious overcompensation for a basic introversion and vice versa. Only specialized psychologists are capable of determining the real character and typic structures of such people and offering wise counsel with respect to a suitable profession in life. Many important forms of testing have been developed to resolve difficulties of this nature. Successful as they have proved to be, however, we must be careful not to accept them uncritically. Not all facets of the personality can be measured. Furthermore, the choice of a profession should not be made solely in terms of the individual's desires and talents; concrete social possibilities should also be taken into consideration. In Western society, for example, anyone who manifests a desire and the talent for technology, science, teaching, or medicine can generally be encouraged to follow his natural inclinations. But when it becomes a question of a literary or artistic career, more than desire and talent are required. To have a serious chance of succeeding one should be superiorly endowed.

I would frankly discourage anyone from making writing his principal occupation unless he had proved that he has a reasonable chance of lasting success. Too many young authors, after the success of a first novel, have wasted their talent and lived in the most painful insecurity. To subsist they write indiscriminately for journals and reviews without always having anything to say. They would be much better off and literature would benefit if they wrote less and made a living in some other professional activity. Among the best writers we find many professors, journalists, doctors, even civil servants and engineers.

# 4

# *Social Life*

In Chapter 1 we spoke about the mission and social responsibilities of the *intelligentsia*. We must now note that the
intellectual is also an individual and as a result is entitled to
certain pleasures.

There have been outstanding examples of scientists and
artists who fled society to live in isolation. Solitude seemed to
be a necessary condition of their intellectual creativity. But
most intellectuals have neither the strength nor the desire to
live this way. The solitary is likely to become a victim of
neurasthenia; he also risks cutting himself off from the real
problems and needs of mankind and becoming an ivory-
tower intellectual interested only in the pure essences of
things without concern for their social repercussions. The
"pure intellectual" may not need social contact for the
fecundity of his work. But for others social relations, provided they are not indulged in excessively, can be an excellent stimulus. Celebrated scholars (a prehistorian and a
biologist, to mention but two) have told me that they derive
great profit from conversations with their colleagues as well

as laymen. I have personally found this to be true. Many of my ideas for books come from such encounters because they give me an opportunity to find out what people are thinking and what problems need clarifying. Likewise, a professor who lives in constant contact with other men, his colleagues, students, and friends, is generally distinguished from a recluse by the concrete and living quality of his teaching.

The value of social relations is incontestable. But they are not all equally beneficial. Some can be very harmful both to the intellectual's work and his personality.

The most superficial and least fruitful form of social life is, without doubt, the cocktail party. Almost everyone feels obliged to give or attend such parties, but scarcely anyone derives any benefit from them. The cocktail party is a typical example of the enslaving power of modern social life. It is easy to drink too much and eat unhealthy food; what is worse, the contacts we make are by the nature of things fleeting and uninteresting. One flits about making a few light remarks to this or that person without entering into serious conversation with anyone. The only thing that could conceivably justify a cocktail party is the hope of meeting someone we are interested in but would not be likely to meet elsewhere.

Given the present mores of social life, at least in the big cities, most professional people would probably find it hard to avoid cocktail parties. It is sometimes alleged that avoiding them could result in quick oblivion for a promising or even a well-established talent. In that case one would be wise to keep such sorties to a strict minimum. Discipline in this matter is all the more imperative in that there exists a real danger of "cocktailomania." I know intellectuals of considerable promise who wouldn't think of missing a cocktail party. They are bored by them, criticize them bitterly, but if they are not invited (especially when they know the time and place it is being given) they are genuinely frustrated and feel that something important is passing them by. This mania is encountered more frequently among intellectual women than men, and especially among the wives of intellectuals. The latter are under the erroneous impression of belonging to the intellectual elite because the cocktail party affords them the opportunity of exchanging a few words with a fashionable writer, a celebrated artist, or a well-known politician. In fact, they are for the most part wasting their time and hurting their health. I know many of them who have, as a result of too many such parties, become alcoholics and even derelicts.

Another form of social life, particularly popular in France, is dinner parties. They are far superior to cocktail parties, especially if the hostess is intelligent enough to invite compatible people who have something to say to one another. There is a real art to being a hostess where intellectuals are concerned. Some wives of public figures are marvelous public relations agents for their husbands. Let me point out to them, if I might, that it is not always desirable to invite professors with professors, doctors with doctors, novelists with novelists, and so forth. Social encounters between members of the same profession are dull more often than pleasurable. One hostess I know thought it a good idea to invite psychiatrists and psychotherapists. The conversation was cool and consisted mostly of banalities. Then they began to talk shop and the conversation soon degenerated into violent arguments. One guest took sharp issue with another's methods and ideas; another made a rapid exit; still another withdrew into morbid silence. Things are not always that bad, of course. Not all intellectuals are as sectarian or fanatic as many practitioners of psychology. Nonetheless a writer, for example, is likely to derive more profit from a conversation with engineers or doctors than from his peers. The same is generally true for other professions as well.

When an intellectual is invited he can assume that others want to get to know him. It is therefore normal for him to reveal himself in talking about his ideas, his work, and what concerns him in life. But that does not give him the right to monopolize the conversation. It is boring, particularly at a dinner party, to listen to long monologues. Other guests might like to make themselves known and shine a bit. Moreover, those who are inclined to talk a lot can generally profit from listening to others, for however educated one may be there is always something to learn from contact with other human beings.

Good manners often dictate that subjects like religion, politics, and racism not be brought up at social gatherings. Since the Nazi atrocities in particular people tend to be extremely discreet about the Jews, so much so that sometimes the mere fact of being Jewish is insurance against any form of criticism. But it seems to me, in this era of ecumenism, that there should be no taboo subjects. Educated men should be able to discuss their religious or political differences without giving offense. It is my experience that conversation on ideological themes interests just about everyone. Moreover, today there is much less fanaticism than, say, a quarter of a century ago.

As soon as an intellectual has achieved some fame he is likely to be invited to dinner as often as to cocktail parties. Many dine out every evening. Which means that they regularly eat, talk, and drink too much and retire late. Consequently their time for reading and reflection suffers. A young novelist of talent became a popular party intellectual as a result of winning a prestigious prize. Since then he hasn't read one worthwhile book. That was almost ten years ago. At first he was able to rest on his laurels, but in the past few years his novels offer nothing to his readers, being little more than a clever combination of the tricks of his trade and the exploitation of what he believes to be public taste. Even his most fervent admirers are beginning to weary of him. At parties he is no longer capable of contributing anything to a serious conversation. He is content to play the role of a high society raconteur.

It would obviously be a mistake to set arbitrary limitations to an intellectual's social life. But it is a good rule of thumb to frequent purely social gatherings as little as possible. I cannot but approve of those who limit such occasions to once a week. Their health and work both benefit.

Another form of social life is professional membership in a club. In the not too distant past most intellectuals affected a fierce individualism and wouldn't dream of grouping together like the workers. They preferred resignation or anarchist revolt in misery to the struggle for bettering the conditions of life. Today doctors, lawyers, writers, teachers, and artists all have their professional organizations. These deal with the public authorities, sign collective contracts, and the like. True, one is free to join or not to join such organizations in democratic countries. But since those who are not members generally profit from the organization anyway, it seems to me that they have a moral duty to join.

In addition, many intellectuals organize for religious or political reasons. There are centers for Catholic scientists, a union of progressive writers, an association of Protestant university professors and so forth. Members of such clubs number writers of every discipline and nationality. Each of these movements also organizes annual conventions both on the national and international levels. Some intellectuals also find it profitable to belong to associations that group together men of different professions and beliefs. Rotary clubs would be an example of this, where writers, doctors, professors, artists, and businessmen meet and share ideas.

These national and international encounters are of great value. Friendships are cemented, one becomes acquainted with what others are doing, and common thinking is brought to bear on professional problems. But here as elsewhere certain limits must be observed. If a famous intellectual accepted all the invitations he received to speak at these gatherings (all of which are interesting in themselves) he would scarcely have time to do any work. Some I know have almost become professional convention-goers, spending more time at them than at work. I do not deny that they do much good, but the evidence indicates that they should not be imitated by those who are serious about their profession. It seems to me safe to say that not more than one evening per week should be given to such organizations. If this rule were observed one could profitably belong to one or even two associations. Likewise, one international convention per year seems sufficient, unless of course we happen to be an official of the organization. Otherwise we disperse our energies. In an age that is so concerned with efficiency we must be less guided by "honors" than by the more genuine services we are capable of rendering.

What norm should be followed in choosing one or another organization? This depends on individual circumstances. In some countries a Catholic doctor, for example, is for all practical purposes obliged to belong to an organization of Catholic doctors. In others, a Protestant writer could scarcely succeed in his profession unless he belonged to an analogous association. But it is probable that the present wave of ecumenism will break down these rigid guidelines. For my part, I prefer to meet with colleagues from different countries as well as different religious, political, and professional tendencies. I find this more enriching than meeting with those who think and believe as I do. But, as I said earlier, to each his own.

# 5

# *Mens Sana in Corpore Sano*

There was a time when intellectuals thought they had some kind of obligation to abuse their bodies and health. The world *hygiene* horrified them. Their study was expected to be dirty or at least disordered. They dressed poorly, drank little, and were ashamed to eat their fill. The common conception of the intellectual was of a man with an emaciated face, long, uncombed hair, and frail limbs. Health was considered an obstacle to fruitful intellectual work. When I was young I often heard doubt cast on the intellectual integrity of a given professor or writer for the simple reason that he dressed well and appeared to be in excellent health. Although perhaps not consciously aware of it, such intellectuals held to certain ideas about asceticism which they wrongly believed to be Christian. Over the centuries, Christian asceticism often forgot the fundamental dogma of Christianity which is the mystery of the Incarnation, an event which once and for all sanctified matter in general and the body in particular. Obscure Neo-Platonic and Gnostic influences inspired contempt for the body in great numbers of candidates for spiritual perfection. They reduced the body to slavery so that the spirit could be freer. Christian people came to look upon an unhealthy body as one of the most evident marks of sanctity. Well-fed monks were maliciously satirized. Charlatans were experts at turning this mentality to their advantage. They long capitalized on the Manichean duality between body and soul to promote a disembodied kind of spirituality. I am thinking of a young atheist intellectual of fine physique. He is ashamed of it before his friends, feels guilty and is making every effort to ruin his exceptionally good health. Although not particularly fond of alcohol, for example, he forced himself to overindulge. Again, while he did his best work in the morning, he kept late hours in an effort to imitate what he took to be a model intellectual. He was quite happy and proud when he eventually contracted tuberculosis. Only after great resistance did he agree to accept treatment.

Happily those days are gone. Even Christian ascetics are beginning to admit that an intense spiritual life in no way requires one to enslave the body. From another point of view, depth psychology has made it clear that any form of slavery leads to a violent effort to achieve freedom. Nothing is more negatively destructive than the insurrection of slaves. Most genuine intellectuals admit this. Few any longer believe in the famous theory of "compensation" according to which a great mind could only thrive in a sickly body. We know that Blaise Pascal, for example, had poor health. But scarcely anyone today would argue that this was the cause or the condition of his genius. Many other creative minds combined a robust health and scholarly achievement. In any case, intellectuals today need not be ashamed of a well-nourished and muscled body or fear to engage in sports and observe the basic rules of hygiene. Juvenal's celebrated maxim—*mens sana in corpore sano*—now has a place of honor. Almost everywhere university professors, for example, are members of athletic clubs. Only pseudo-intellectuals, and especially pseudo-artists, still affect an unkempt exterior in the false hope of convincing the public of their authenticity.

Still, despite the progress we have just been talking about, the modern intellectual must make an effort to achieve a balance between body and soul. Prejudices have disappeared but the conditions of modern life often play almost as harmful a role. Thus it seems to me in order to discuss this matter in some detail and offer some practical advice.

## THE SEDENTARY LIFE AND OVERWORK

Most intellectuals lead an excessively sedentary life. They remain long hours seated at a desk and thus risk seriously endangering their health. They are inclined to overweight and are often obese before they are forty. The spinal cord and vertebrae become distorted. Constipation is a chronic threat, bringing with it constant discomforts and an appreciable diminution in one's working capacity. After forty the blood pressure rises at an alarming rate, endangering not only health but life itself. Many intellectuals die prematurely of heart attacks without having made their potential contribution to the human community.

In addition to the dangers of a sedentary life there are those of overwork. While manual laborers rarely exceed a forty-hour week, and sometimes work less than thirty hours, most intellectuals go way beyond these limits. Many corporation presidents, doctors, and researchers work more than ten hours a day. And intellectual work is at least as tiring as manual labor. Less muscular energy is expended, to be sure, but the output of nervous energy is far greater. And nervous fatigue is without question more serious than muscular fatigue and far more difficult to treat.

Early sexual impotence is one of the frequent consequences of intellectual overwork. The files of neurologists, psychotherapists, and general practitioners are full of such cases. This is a serious matter. If sexuality could easily be separated from the totality of psychic life, an impotent man could say with some justification: "Good riddance." But in fact, the loss of sexual virility almost inevitably brings about the loss of virility as such. Those who are impotent lose interest in work, discourage easily, become morose, ineffectively aggressive, and age prematurely. Consequently even the man who lives, by reason of his vocation or by force of circumstances, in complete chastity must still consider sexual impotence an evil and seek to remedy it.

Intellectuals are inclined to have more fragile psyches than other men. Sometimes this fragility is constitutional; sometimes it is the result of overstrain on the brain, the center of all psychic activity. I realize, of course, that the real causes of neuroses must be sought in the traumas of childhood and adolescence. But in many cases we may suppose that had the patient led a less tense life the neurosis would never have surfaced.

A frequent cause of overwork and psychic exhaustion among intellectuals is excessive ambition. We noted earlier how important ambition is for success in life, but it must be proportioned to our ability. All men are not equally endowed with energy. Someone could be exceptionally gifted intellectually but psychically fragile. He might rightly think that what he does is in accordance with his intellectual capacity. As a result his failure scandalizes and discourages him. He doesn't see why he can't work twelve hours a day when a colleague who is not superior to him intellectually can do so without any difficulty. It is my experience that many neurotic intellectuals can be cured only on condition that they agree to change radically their way of life and work habits. They must convince themselves that they are not incurable invalids or cripples simply because they must curb their ambition.

Henry is a forty-year-old engineer. He has average intelligence and an excellent appetite. Since he graduated he has held a number of positions, all of which he had to leave because of professional incompetence. Logically, such incompetence didn't make sense. After his last failure he came to see me in a serious state of psychic and nervous exhaustion. He slept little, cried easily and had no self-confidence at all. He felt completely washed up. Psychotherapy enabled Henry to return to work. He found a well-paying job with good hours. But it soon became evident to me that he was courting further failure. Not so much because of mistakes, this time, but rather because he wanted to do too much. He felt inferior to one of his classmates who had been promoted and wanted to equal his performance. He thought that he might do so by making an excellent impression and working non-stop. The results were all too predictable: because of constant tension and overwork his work was only mediocre, although quite in line with his actual talents. He can only be cured if he agrees to set a limit to his ambitions and understands that his aggravating inferiority complex is the direct result of misjudging his real talents.

## FALSE CURES

Many intellectuals are perfectly aware of their dangerous work habits and make some effort to correct them. Unfortunately the cure is often worse than the disease.

In the first place, they often have too frequent recourse to medication. I know a writer who works far into the night drinking cup after cup of black coffee and smoking cigarette after cigarette. When he eventually retires he has to take a strong dose of sleeping pills. When he wakes up next morning, poorly rested after an artificial sleep, he resorts to energy pills. It is obvious that this kind of regime makes intolerable demands on the nervous system.

Others seek relaxation in alcohol, driving at high speed, or gambling. Again it is evident that these efforts are equally ineffective. They never result in health or balance and often lead to a total nervous breakdown, even suicide.

But the intellectual is not condemned to an impoverished life and early death. These can be avoided if he remembers at all times that the body is the necessary vehicle of the spirit, that psychic health is difficult to achieve without physical health. If he has little taste for physical exercise he mustn't deceive himself by pretending that all great men were physically weak. True, men like Pascal, Dostoevsky, Toulouse-Lautrec, and others deserve our admiration for having produced masterpieces despite poor health. But we must never forget that it was not *because* of their infirmities but *in spite* of them that they succeeded. The strength of their minds overcame the weakness of their bodies. Their example should be a source of encouragement for those who are physically afflicted. But it would be presumptuous to point to these exceptional cases as an excuse for deliberately neglecting our bodily health.

## SLEEP

The first indispensable requisite for good health is sleep. As regrettable as the fact that we must pass a good part of our short lives in an unconscious state may be, it is unavoidable. We must resign ourselves to the realities of our human condition. Moreover, depth psychology has discovered that the hours spent in sleep contribute to our intellectual creativity. As the Bible says, while the body sleeps the spirit remains vigilant. Not only does sleep restore the energy we need when we are awake, it is also a time of maturation. Descartes is not the only one to have received the basic insight into his philosophical system while asleep.

Different individuals need different amounts of sleep. An average of eight hours per night is recommended, but some can get by on six while others need as much as ten hours. Generally an extra hour is needed in winter time. A young man needs less sleep than the mature while the aged need less than the young. Nervous temperaments need the most sleep while the choleric and the sanguine need the least. Lack of energy or interest in life cause some people to sleep longer. If we lose sleep one night it should be made up for the next. But even the very healthy should guard against losing sleep several nights in a row. This would necessarily result in some disorder or other.

It is desirable to retire early. Experts have observed that sleep during the first part of the night is the most restful. The ideal would be to sleep from eleven to seven or, better still, from ten to six o'clock. But these are only general guidelines. As the popular saying has it: it all depends on one's temperament. As a rule, the habits formed in childhood last a lifetime. Here again, each must follow his own rhythm. But it may be stated categorically that the practice some intellectuals have of working all night and sleeping during the day is very harmful to the health.

Sleeping pills should be avoided if at all possible. They are always damaging to the nervous system. They are habit-forming and can become veritable poisons. They should be used only in exceptional circumstances as a means of procuring the necessary minimum of sleep. Many habitual users of soporifics are anxiety-ridden and are afraid to go to sleep any other way. When they can be persuaded to do without them they are frequently agreeably surprised to find that sleep comes quite naturally and is far more restful.

If one has difficulty sleeping there are more natural and effective remedies than drugs. A short walk, gymnastics, exercises, a shower, or a cup of tea are a few of the natural remedies that have proved helpful.

## PHYSICAL EXERCISE

Sociologists and psychologists rightly call work that demands only physical effort "dehumanizing." Assembly-line work in particular has been criticized. With modern technical progress (electronics, cybernetics, etc.) more and more purely physical labor is being taken over by machines. Theoretically we can envisage a day when work will be more "human" but in practice that time is still a long way off.

But exclusively intellectual work is equally dehumanizing. The standard caricature of the intellectual—bald head, thick glasses, thin chest, and spindly legs—is just as mutilated a human being as the most servile of manual laborers. Intellectual activity should go hand in hand with a minimum of physical exercise. With a little effort most intellectuals could exercise their bodies just as easily as their minds.

I heartily approve the example of those intellectuals who live in the country and spend a few hours each day gardening, cutting wood, and engaging in similar forms of manual labor. Experience proves that this kind of life enhances intellectual endeavor. One writer I know who leads such a life writes very bracing novels, and I suspect this is in no small part due to the fact that he lives in the full sense of the word, while authors of "underground" novels generally find their inspiration in the factitious atmosphere of smoke-filled cafés. Another well-known philosopher of my acquaintance has built a workshop in his garage and spends several hours a day in it. But not all intellectuals can live in the country, nor are all gifted with manual dexterity. But all of them need physical exercise. A strict minimum would be fifteen minutes of gymnastics each morning and evening and a brisk half-hour walk each day. Unfortunately most of us are obliged to take our daily walks along city streets where the air is polluted and the noise deafening. But this is better than nothing, especially if it is complemented by a weekly sojourn in the country.

The so-called Swedish gymnastics, with emphasis on breathing and body relaxation, seem to me imperative for those intellectuals who are not athletically inclined. They should be practiced regularly before an open window. More recent methods of relaxation (for example that of Schultz) are especially beneficial for nervous temperaments. But for maximum effectiveness they should be carried out under the supervision of a specialist.

Yoga has been widely practiced in the West of late. But I cannot recommend it without certain reservations. The Hindus themselves have similar reservations about the usefulness of yoga for Westerners. They point out that yoga is not merely a physical exercise but an integral part of a spirituality and ascesis, and the two cannot be separated without serious dangers. In any case yoga should never be undertaken without a competent and conscientious guide. Otherwise it can lead to various physical and psychic disturbances. Moreover, many so-called masters of yoga are charlatans. They don't seriously follow the prescriptions of real yoga and exploit a popular fad.

Sports like swimming and tennis are, of course, to be encouraged at all times. I know one reputable intellectual who has a "black belt" in judo. Too, the intellectual must always be careful not to overexert himself. The greater part of his energy must after all be expended in mental activities. In general, physical exercise should be considered a distraction, a means to an end rather than an end in itself.

## RELAXATION

Intellectual work imposes great tension on the mind and nervous system. Under pain of nervous exhaustion and sometimes serious psychic illness, it is absolutely mandatory to provide for release of this tension. Those engaged in intellectual work must be convinced of the primacy of quality over quantity and the impossibility of doing anything worthwhile when overworked or fatigued. To avoid both of the latter conditions the intellectual must find a happy balance between work and relaxation.

The advice given in the preceding paragraphs will procure a certain amount of relaxation. In addition, everyone exercising an intellectual profession should take one day a week off. There is something incongruous in interpreting the Church's precept concerning the Sabbath in such a way that forbids women to sew on Sunday but permits the professor or writer to carry on as usual. The intellectual needs a weekly break as much as the laborer or farmer. Sundays should be given over to family life, physical exercise, and light reading. Nothing is more pernicious than the habit of bringing week-end work home. One returns to the office on Monday morning as tired as when one left on Friday. And the accumulation of tension and fatigue can have serious consequences. Teachers should organize their work so as to leave Sunday free. At all costs intellectuals should avoid the example of those American businessmen who work until they are exhausted, take a cure at some clinic for two or three months, return to their former pace and then to the clinic again the following year. Under these conditions the day will soon come when therapy will be unable to help them. It is no coincidence that a high percentage of intellectuals die prematurely of heart disease between the ages of forty and fifty-five.

We have already pointed out that racing is one of the false forms of relaxation. Frequenting the cabarets and casinos is scarcely better.

Nor should we be satisfied with relaxing only on Sundays and during vacations. We must take measures to ward off tension during working hours as well. Thus it is desirable not to spend too long doing the same thing. Only the exceptionally robust are capable of concentrating on one thing for more than four hours. One should have several projects going at once, for a change in this case is often as good as a rest. With a little foresight and organization this kind of relaxation can be had in almost all intellectual professions. It is also wise to do our hardest work in the morning when we are in top form. Otherwise it will worry us all day and prevent us from doing the secondary, mechanical tasks well. And when we realize at the end of the day that important work remains to be done we feel guilty and are tempted to prolong the working day or take a full briefcase home with us.

It is important to leave off work at the normal time even though we have to put off until tomorrow what we intended to do today. I know one company president who goes home when his employees do. In the evening he plays with his children, helps his wife in the kitchen, and reads the papers or a book that has nothing to do with his professional interests. The economist might find relaxation in books on philosophy or religion, while one of my novelist friends relaxes by reading in the field of mathematics and physics.

Relaxation should never be sought in drugs. They merely give the illusion that we can work more than we actually can.

The benefits of the relaxation we have been discussing here are largely preventive. This advice is not applicable to those who are already psychically exhausted. In that case professional treatment is called for. But the effects of treatment will endure only as long as the laws of mental hygiene are strictly adhered to.

## FOOD AND DRINK

One of the paradoxes of our age is the fact that a good half of mankind is undernourished while the prosperous countries of the West are overfed. In both the United States and Western Europe we eat too much; a good many diseases can be traced directly to this. Perhaps some of our excesses in this respect are a reaction against the restrictions and frustrations we experienced during the last war. Consumption of meat in particular has greatly increased. Most families now eat meat twice a day whereas in France they were lucky to have it twice a week in 1940. Such rich food might be safely eaten by manual workers; but it is altogether unhealthy for sedentary intellectuals.

Dieticians estimate that laborers should consume about 3000 calories a day, while 2000–2400 is quite enough for intellectuals. But the number of calories is only an approximate indication. It is equally important to work out a well-balanced diet, both qualitatively and quantitatively.

The science of dietetics has made much progress in the past few decades. Systems elaborated by Paul Carton and Gaye-lord Hauser, for example, have been among the most popular with the public. They have much in common. Both encourage a "natural" diet which would exclude industrially processed foods such as canned goods. Carton is more of a vegetarian. He is against red wine and all forms of pork, and only under exceptional circumstances does he approve of white wine and chicken or veal. He also disapproves of all foods that have nitrogen or acid in them. Thus he recommends that we eat few eggs, no fish or such fruits and vegetables as oranges, lemons, and tomatoes. The American dietician Gayelord Hauser promises a longer life to those who select their food on the basis of vitamins. He strongly recommends wheat germ, skim milk, yeast, molasses and yogurt as well as vegetable and fruit juices. Nor does he consider tomatoes, oranges, and lemons to be dangerous.

I am not going to recommend any special dietetic system. The recommendations of both Carton and Hauser have been highly successful in alleviating skin diseases, hepatitis, and some forms of arthritis. I have also been able to verify the psychic advantages of a "natural" diet. But I do not approve of vegetarianism; it seems to me too fanatical. Vegetarians tend to elevate their dietary systems to a kind of religion outside of which there is no salvation. In the first place, most people cannot procure a sufficient variety of fresh vegetables the year round. To prohibit manufactured foods frequently results in an improper diet. Too, the phobia against acids deprives vegetarians of some of the foods that are richest in vitamins such as tomatoes and oranges. Moreover, red wine is not as injurious as many of Carton's followers hold it to be. The vegetarian belief that consumption of red meat will make men cruel and pork will make them unmannerly has no scientific basis whatsoever. Vegetarian Hindus can be just as cruel as the meat-eating peoples of Europe. And Moslems who do not eat pork are no more mannerly than Northern peoples.

From what I have been able to observe personally a strict "natural" diet has much to recommend it. But it has many disadvantages as well. It seems to me that a dietetic regime should be considered a form of therapy. It is normal to take medication when we are ill; but it would be harmful to the health to make constant use of medications under the pretext of avoiding sickness. On the other hand, some rules of hygiene must be observed with respect to food. This is a matter of elementary prudence.

In observing that many intellectuals eat too much and irrationally, thus harming both their health and their work, I have no intention of condemning them to strict observance of any given regime. It is one of the aberrant tendencies of our times to go from one extreme to the other. I have nothing against carrot juice or yeast; but I find it difficult to believe that the only function of eating is to satisfy the demands of our bodies. Man is more than a well-ordered machine. Eating should also be a pleasure. Moreover, in almost all civilizations it has been regarded as an eminent social act. My advice, particularly to intellectuals, is moderation where food is concerned. A person in good health can eat anything but not too much. He can even permit himself certain excesses, but not every day.

One big meal a day seems to me adequate for those not engaged in physical labor. Normally it should be eaten in the middle of the day, although this is often difficult under the conditions of urban living. It is also desirable for the whole family to gather at the table at least once a day; this is often the only occasion when they can all be together. The evening is usually the most suitable time for such a meal, when the parents and children have finished their normal duties. It is also the most convenient time to invite friends.

The habit of eating late at night is bad for both digestion and a good night's sleep. The main meal should be eaten no later than seven o'clock. This also has the advantage of leaving the evening free. Ideally, entertainment should begin no later than eight o'clock to enable people to get home at a reasonable hour. Of course, I am aware that people are not likely to change their habits overnight. But some improvements in our eating habits seem imperative. Many intelligent people, in the interests of their health, have had to give up going out during the week and invite guests only on Saturday evening.

The French, in particular, would do well to change their breakfast habits. Since it is no longer as a rule possible to eat the main meal in the middle of the day, by the same token a light breakfast is no longer sufficient. Dieticians recommend that breakfast include toast, butter, jams, cheese, an egg, and fresh fruit. This kind of breakfast eliminates the need for meat or wine at lunch. At this time a plate of vegetables, cheese, and fruit should suffice. Many people settle for a sandwich. This system would enable people to work in a steady fashion during the day and get home earlier in the evening.

The main dinner dish should be preceded by a small

amount of soup or hors d'oeuvres. Raw tomatoes, rich in vitamin C, are particularly recommended to intellectuals. They shouldn't eat too much meat. Fats and nitrogen are found in abundance in cheese. For dessert fruit is always preferable to sweets. All dieticians recommend that we drink only after we have eaten. In any case, intellectuals should never drink more than a half bottle of wine per meal. And here, too, quality is to be preferred to quantity.

The foregoing recommendations apply to our normal diets. But there are occasions when a little splurging is in order. Even monks take an occasional holiday from the monotony of daily frugality. Intellectuals are no exception. The joys of the spirit alone are not enough for the good life. Parties and banquets are excellent things in themselves. But they are frequently abused. Some businessmen go to official dinners almost every day and some well-known intellectuals accept frequent dinner engagements. We have already pointed out the dangerous consequences of such abuses.

It is obviously difficult to establish precise norms in this matter. I don't think that as a general rule more than one banquet (and/or party) a week is to be recommended. And the day after such an occasion should be more abstemious than usual. Indulgence on festive occasions often adds as much as five pounds to our weight. It should be taken off as soon as possible.

I often advise those of my patients who have liver trouble or nervous stomachs to overindulge occasionally. They perhaps won't feel so well the next day. But while a strict diet may be beneficial for the body it can often have a negative effect on one's morale, making one depressed and anxious. Fanatic proponents of dietetic strictness often forget that food serves not only a physiological function but a psychic one as well. Here as elsewhere we must strive for a happy balance between the body and soul.

I don't mean to ridicule vegetarians or those who renounce alcohol and tobacco. I merely take offense at their sectarianism. I see no a priori reason to forbid intellectuals to smoke or drink wine. This is a source of relaxation and pleasure that can increase their professional effectiveness and contribute to their emotional stability. Here again, moderation is the key. Because intellectual activity demands a great output of nervous energy, intellectuals are more tempted than others to seek compensation in stimulants. In my opinion a dozen cigarettes a day is a good mean. In view of recent statistics on cancer and cigarette smoking it is advisable to smoke a pipe or cigars and under no circumstances inhale.

The first rule to observe with respect to alcohol is never to drink alone. A daily cocktail is much more likely to result in alcoholism than several social drinks. The so-called Irish habit (widely practiced in other lands as well) of drinking glass after glass with the intention of getting intoxicated is for obvious reasons disastrous. The desire to lose consciousness, especially in an educated man, is incontestably neurotic.

# 6

# *Emotional Balance*

## ATROPHY OF THE HEART

However great intellectuals we are or think we are, we must never forget that we are men first of all, subject to the same problems, the same laws of growth, and the same basic responsibilities as other men. We noted in the preceding chapter how important it is for the servant of truth to take care of his body. Equally important is man's emotional life, his capacity for love or the lack thereof.

We often meet highly intelligent men who are emotional dwarfs, still entangled in the conflicts of adolescence. Sometimes the emotional immaturity of an intellectual is greater than that of a non-intellectual of the same age, the same social background and the same education. I know outstanding university professors who at thirty or forty years of age are incapable of loving a woman; some of them have never even experienced the need for love. When they marry they do so for social reasons; the choice of a spouse is motivated by infantile impulses, frequently based on an ideal mother image. Still other intellectuals are incapable of authentic friendship with other men.

An explanation for such retardation can be found in the fact that the intellectual's psychic energy is totally mobilized in the work of the spirit so that he has little left for emotional activities. In reality the same psychic energy nourishes all of our faculties—those of knowing as well as those of willing and loving. If we expend too much in one domain we will not have enough for others. Because psychic energy, like physical energy in this respect, is unevenly distributed among individuals, some can engage in intense intellectual activity without adverse effect upon their emotional life while with others the opposite will be the case. I know few people whose intellectual life was as intense and fruitful as that of my recently deceased friend Emmanuel. He wrote books, edited an important journal, was an intellectual leader among the young (to whom he consecrated a number of hours each day) and, in addition, participated in various intellectual organizations. And few men led so rich and expressive an emotional life. He was a good husband and father and enjoyed a wide range of friendships. To all appearances his rich emotional life increased his intellectual productivity and vice versa. In his case energy circulated freely between the head and the heart.

On the other hand, many professors, scientists, and writers are so emotionally dried up that they are incapable of either love or friendship. Thus Charles, a well-known physicist, at the age of fifty had never had a friend. He even insisted that he never felt the need to have one; love of science satisfied him. He married at thirty-five because, since his mother died, he needed a woman to take care of his material needs. He had no emotional communication whatsoever with either his wife or his children. Nothing but physics interested him and, because he had not been able to interest his family in his work, he had nothing to say to them. Mark, a lawyer and writer, led a life that was equally impoverished emotionally. He didn't even marry, fearing that the intrusion of another person in his life would create an insurmountable obstacle to intellectual creativity. His only satisfying sexual relations were with prostitutes. With them, he argued, there were no emotional complications or commitment. He was not fond of nature, music, or any other form of art. His pleasures were purely cerebral.

As we said, in many cases emotional atrophy is the result of excessive expenditure of energy in intellectual pursuits. A young man can become so interested in, say, a scientific discipline that nothing else matters to him and his energies are totally directed to study and research. But we often note in analysis the inverse—that is, emotional atrophy—is the cause of excessive intellectual activity. Thus Charles' mother had always been a semi-invalid and gave him little affection. His father had been a taciturn and rather strict man. Scarcely had his wife been laid to rest when he set up house-keeping with his long-time mistress in whom Charles clearly saw his mother's rival. He had nothing but contempt for her. At an early age he sought in books escape from a reality that was in the main painful for him. During his secondary studies he was little interested in literature, philosophy, or any discipline that dealt with human problems. Only physics and mathematics attracted him because they did not disturb his repressed emotions.

It sometimes happens that excessive interest in intellectual matters, caused by emotional repression, emerges after adolescence as a result of a traumatic experience. This happened

in the case of the philosopher Robert. Until about the age of
seventeen his life was well balanced. On every count, his
emotions were healthy. One day he chanced to see his mother
in the arms of her lover. From then on he began to despise
the body and the emotions. He decided to become "some-
body" in the intellectual world and, without being aware of
the traumatic motives of his decision, cut all emotional ties
with his friends and relatives on the pretext that only thus
could he serve truth. He succeeded in what he set out to do
but his philosophy was a rigid rationalism. At about the age
of forty he realized the harm he had inflicted upon himself.
The violent emotional outbursts he then indulged in were
clearly puerile in character. For example, he became irre-
sistibly attracted to very young girls and was the laugh-
ingstock of his students. His jealousies were romantically
adolescent and led him eventually to the brink of suicide.

However eminent the intellectual, he cannot be a whole
man unless there is an equilibrium between his intelligence
and emotions. Intellectual creativity itself normally presup-
poses such an equilibrium. One wonders whether it may not
be because so many servants of truth have repressed their
emotions to become merely calculating minds that science
and modern technology have brought more misfortune than
happiness to mankind.

## CHASTITY OR PROMISCUITY?

For centuries there was controversy over whether clerics
should marry or remain celibate. Both the Reform and the
Orthodox Churches favor marriage for their ministers, while
the Roman Church demands strict observance of chastity.
But at Vatican Council II many bishops asked for at least a

partial abolition of a law that seems inhuman to most of our contemporaries. True, the partisans of a married clergy do not as a rule base their arguments on human maturity but rather see in celibacy the cause of both the quantitative and qualitative decrease in vocations. But it is nonetheless possible that the popularization of certain Freudian theses has had a more or less conscious influence on them.

We are not concerned here with the specific problem of the clergy. They interest us only insofar as they may be considered the precursors of our modern intelligentsia.

It is incontestably one of the merits of modern depth psychology to have made clear—albeit not without exaggeration —the primordial role of sexuality in the totality of human life. Normal sexual evolution is seen as indispensable not only for the physical health of the individual but for psychic and emotional fulfillment as well. As proof of this, an impotent person is as a rule incapable of oblative love whether for God or neighbor and his intellectual efficacy itself suffers. The Roman Church, her long contempt for the carnal notwithstanding, forbids the castration of clerics. Origen, one of the brightest thinkers of early Christianity, was held in discredit for centuries, not so much because of his doctrinal errors but because in an exalted moment he castrated himself. A depth psychologist would not hesitate to recommend treatment for an impotent person even if he intended to remain celibate.

Normal sexual development should not be identified with genital activity. If in the past purist prejudices, which held that sexual activity was unworthy of a superior man, had to be combated today we must protest the no less dangerous prejudice which argues that chastity is impossible or at least an obstacle to human fulfillment. Psychoanalysis must bear a good share of responsibility for propagating this reversed taboo. From revindicating the legitimate place of sexual love, Freud, his disciples, and especially his popularizers, gradually went on to postulate the absolute necessity of such love. There are still doctors and psychologists (although fewer in number than thirty years ago) who recommend adultery or periodic visits to prostitutes for patients who suffer from anxiety and obsession. But in fact, this problem is more complex than modern worshipers of Sexus are willing to admit.

There is no doubt that sexuality consumes a great deal of psychic energy. The more such energy, called libido in this case, a man has, the more imperious will his sexual impulses normally be. It would certainly be very dangerous to repress this energy or not provide adequate outlet for it. It would soon break through whatever barriers were erected against it. Obsessions and hallucinations, various perversions and odious crimes represent some of the anarchic eruptions of repressed sexual energy. There is no doubt that this kind of negative chastity must be condemned in the name of spiritual hygiene. It is dangerous and immoral to prohibit the normal use of sexual energy without paying close attention to what will become of the unused energy.

On the other hand there is no objection to positive chastity when it is practiced for the purpose of distributing the energy normally expended genitally to other psychic activities. Chastity, whether embraced by the secular intellectual or the cleric, has no moral value unless it is viewed as a means of channeling more energy into intellectual or spiritual activities. It is indeed dangerous and immoral when considered an end in itself.

If prolonged chastity in the adult is to be healthy the energies it leaves unused must be *sublimated.* An intense spiritual life, intellectual work, artistic engagement and the like are in varying degrees capable of putting the libidinal energies normally reserved for genital activity to creative use. But we should be under no illusions on this point. Even the most fervent of mystics and the most productive of intellectuals are incapable of sublimating all of their libidinal energies. Some of it will remain invested in the sexual instinct. Complete chastity is therefore almost always very difficult. But experience seems to authorize the opinion that the non-sublimated libidinal energies are scarcely ever of a nature to disrupt the psyche of a genuine intellectual. It can even be a source of superior psychic activity. But, on the other hand, there is no evidence that the intellectual should not lead a normal sexual life. Among the great scientists, writers, and artists, some have practiced total chastity while others married and had families. There is no reason to conclude that one way of life is superior to the other.

Promiscuity is much more dangerous for the intellectual than chastity, even if it is poorly sublimated. Many intellectuals are under the illusion that they can find in promiscuity a release from the tensions brought on by excessive cerebral activity. But this is as self-defeating as overindulgence in alcohol, tobacco, or drugs. In my professional career as a psychotherapist I have encountered many neurotics whose conflicts were closely bound up with the brutal repression of their sexual instincts. But I have encountered an equal number whose neuroses if not strictly caused by sexual overindulgence were at least seriously complicated by it. Highly educated men and women have ruined themselves by promiscuity. All of their psychic energy was "burned up" by their sexual activity and nothing was left for intellectual pursuits.

Doctor T., an esteemed endocrinologist and author of a

number of influential books, was considered by his colleagues to be one of the great hopes of medical science. Until he was thirty he lived in complete chastity and dedicated himself entirely to scientific research. Then he married. But in his ignorance of feminine psychology he chose a wife who was incapable of understanding him. She soon left him. He interpreted this as a sign of the total collapse of his life. He believed that he could overcome this failure only by adopting a way of life diametrically opposed to what he had hitherto known. Thus he became a dedicated seducer and carried on several love affairs at once. At first this intense sexual indulgence seemed to stimulate his intellectual work. But gradually it became a veritable obsession. Mistresses no longer satisfied him; he began frequenting houses of prostitution at regular intervals. He then lost interest in his work; his sexual escapades were accompanied by professional incompetence. Finally he gave up his studies, abandoned himself to immorality and, for all practical purposes, became an outcast.

This is obviously an extreme example. In most cases promiscuity is not so catastrophic. But it always impedes intellectual activity, which requires moderation on the sexual level as well as in food and drink.

## MARRIAGE OR CELIBACY?

Should the intellectual marry in order to find emotional equilibrium? There is no reason why he shouldn't; but, on the other hand, marriage should not be postulated as an a priori condition of personal fulfillment. Each case must be considered on its merits. Individual personalities and vocations have an important bearing on this question. The most we can say is that conjugal love is perhaps less indispensable for the emotional fulfillment of the intellectual than other men because he is more likely to expend his energies in other activities.

Some intellectuals are incapable of taking an active interest in the many details of family life. Worries about their children's health, monetary matters, and the many social obligations of a married man interfere with their work. They cannot be blamed if they refuse to marry. I have friends who remained celibate, not for selfish reasons, but because they knew themselves sufficiently well to realize that it would be difficult if not altogether impossible for them to make a woman happy and assume the responsibilities of fatherhood. When such intellectuals marry anyway, they are more or less unconsciously looking for a maternal wife who can take care of the material tasks of daily life. Many marriages of this sort are highly successful, especially when there are no children. Sometimes, too, intellectuals who are ill at ease in the practical domain seek a disciple in a wife. Her admiration is a source of encouragement for them.

But not all intellectuals are necessarily unsuited for normal family life. Illustrious scholars of all ages have been exemplary husbands and fathers. Family life served as a beneficial relaxation from their work and provided the emotional warmth they needed. Many of them also successfully acquitted themselves of their material responsibilities. The distaste for household chores seems more characteristic of modern intellectuals than their predecessors.

The successful choice of a marriage partner depends on several conditions. There is no reason why an intellectual should seek an intellectual wife. In many cases marriages between intellectuals are unsatisfactory, if not for the parents at least for the children. In such marriages there is good reason to fear that the woman will be no more interested in house-work than the man. But it doesn't follow that the ideal wife for an intellectual be a mere servant. Take the case of Doctor G. Realizing that he was uninterested in practical things and following his mother's advice, he married a woman from a good family who had little schooling but possessed all the qualities of a perfect homemaker. She was intelligent and very much in love with her husband. But despite all the good will in the world she grew periodically infuriated with his habit of buying books when there were so many "more prac-tical" expenses necessary for the upkeep of their home. Her husband's "mania" struck her as all the more inexplicable in that he never read all the books he purchased. Professor L.'s wife left him scarcely a year after they were married because his irregular hours and working habits proved too much of a strain on her middle-class mentality. The judge found this sufficient grounds for divorce.

In general we may say that an intellectual's wife should be sufficiently educated and intelligent to understand her hus-band's right to certain "peculiarities" even though she doesn't share them. In my experience the most successful marriages are between a teacher and a student. It happens often enough that the intellectual, because of long years of study, marries later than the average. And since he generally remains young at heart there seems to be no reason why he should not marry a woman considerably younger than him-self. The wife-disciple, although she may not necessarily be an intellectual, is more capable than anyone of admiring her husband-teacher and tolerating his eccentricities. The oppor-tunity for intense intellectual communication is of a nature to compensate her for the inconveniences of having married an older man. But many intellectuals marry older women.

This is especially true of those who are impractical and emotionally retarded. In a maternal wife they find protection and a feeling of security which they would otherwise lack. She takes charge of the household and frequently works as well. This is often the case when the intellectual is an artist or writer who has not yet been recognized by the public. The disadvantage of this kind of marriage is that the man may never mature.

The intellectual who marries should be prepared to accept the obligations of fatherhood. Moreover, his paternal role can contribute greatly to his own emotional fulfillment and the fecundity of his work. If he becomes more "human" himself his work necessarily benefits. I know writers and professors who are so introverted that they write their books for themselves and give courses without asking whether or not the students will be able to understand them. Fatherhood can be very therapeutic for such types. Every father worthy of the name, and clearly even great intellectuals can be fathers worthy of the name, adapts himself by the force of circumstances to the different phases of intellectual and emotional growth in his children. And thus he becomes more adapted to life in general.

## THE BONDS OF FRIENDSHIP

The intellectual more than other men requires a wide circle of friends for his emotional fulfillment. It pertains to the intellectual to transcend the singular and achieve universality in the emotional as well as the intellectual sense of the word. His love for a few friends and for his wife and children, should expand to embrace mankind as a whole. Great intellectuals of the past have not limited their emotional attachments to family, nation, or race. One has only to recall the international friendships of such men as Leibnitz, Descartes, Malebranche, Goethe, Voltaire, and Einstein. Today, especially, intellectuals of different countries have done themselves honor by daring to publicly oppose national and racial fanaticism, all that divides peoples. Some go yet further and open their hearts to the universe as such.

As we pointed out earlier, it is quite legitimate for the intellectual to renounce marriage and erotic love either because this is demanded by his calling or because he feels incapable of such responsibilities. But this does not mean that he should renounce his emotional fulfillment. This would be to seriously mutilate his very being. Erotic love is one of the ways, in itself an excellent way, to achieve this fulfillment. But it is not the only way. Friendship also serves this purpose, whether as a complement to erotic love or as a function of chastity. There is no vocation that is incompatible with friendship.

More spiritual by its nature, originating not in the excitation of the senses but in serenity and light, there is no danger that friendship will prevent the intellectual from realizing his vocation as erotic love in some cases could. Friendship, like love, is a function of our emotional make-up; it is not always rationally evident why we have one friendship rather than another. But however irrationally motivated, friendship is far more serene than love. Friendship between intellectuals especially is above all an exchange, a communion of minds. It enables them to break out of narcissistic isolation and know another person intimately. A friend appeals to our generosity (even when he asks nothing) and makes his available to us. Friendship is essentially a form of spiritual communion and gives expression to what is most authentic in us. Dialogue between friends is never merely sensual; it is founded on knowledge and the common love of something that transcends individual interests. Friendship enables us to discover new dimensions in our lives, to become aware of our superiority to the smallness and miseries which are the habitual lot of the solitary self. Since generosity is the condition and very essence of friendship, we will soon come to realize that what we possess is far inferior to what we want to give. We must, therefore, continue to grow, and it will be largely due to the generosity of our friends that we will multiply our intellectual and emotional capital. But friendship not only increases our personal treasure; it also promotes our capacity to act.

Sometimes intellectuals have friends who do not share their interest in the things of the mind. It may be a childhood friend, or one encountered during the war and imprisonment. The emotional value of such friendships cannot be doubted; they have the further advantage of bringing the intellectual into existential contact with realities that are more concrete than those he is normally accustomed to. But the most satisfying relationships are with other intellectuals, with men and women who share the same interests. All friendship in the end implies a certain equality.

A particularly satisfying form of emotional fulfillment for the intellectual is the teacher-student relationship. We pointed out in Chapter 2 how important it is for the young intellectual to have a teacher as a model and guide. The choice of a teacher is certainly motivated by intellectual prestige; but emotional affinities play an equally important role. This explains why students choose teachers who are not necessarily the most eminent in their fields. When an intellectual has reached a certain age and acquired a certain reputation he may be lucky enough to have disciples, which is not the same thing as having students. The student learns what the professor teaches without necessarily agreeing with it. But between a teacher and his disciple there is a kind of spiritual relationship, a certain emotional rapport.

Every teacher, however eminent, naturally desires disciples. His prestige should be based on real superiority and he should be able to influence his young disciple so as to bring out the latter's talents and potential. He should renounce all authoritarianism and all spirit of domination, otherwise he will not have disciples and friends but mere followers. Spiritual imperialism is no more desirable than political imperialism; instead of liberating and elevating, it enslaves.

Because reciprocity is essential to all friendship some doubt the possibility of such a relationship between teacher and disciple. It would seem that the teacher gives while the disciple only receives. But this is only apparently the case. Those who may be rightly considered masters, that is those who are aware that they have a mission and a message, considered it a privilege to have disciples, and even more so disciples who are friends. To be surrounded with young men who love him and accept his message with enthusiasm and gratitude can only be a source of great joy for a teacher. He finds in such friendship something like a fountain of youth; and above all he may hope that his message will live on in his disciples. Thus it is that through Plato and other disciples and friends Socrates continues to speak to us twenty-five centuries after his death. A similar phenomenon obtains in the case of Christ.

There are outstanding intellectuals without friends, who in fact are afraid of having them. This is particularly true of those who do research; their narcissism is such that they think any form of communication with others will detract from their work. Some scientists, especially those engaged in the abstract sciences, defend their ideas with such passion and exclusivity that they come to scorn those who do not think exactly as they do. I once attended an international conference of philosophers and psychoanalysts where each participant soliloquized at length without concern for what others thought and made no effort to establish contact with their confreres. Several refused to attend the lectures and left the room after they had spoken their piece. It goes without saying that such men are incapable of friendship or any other emotional relationship. I wouldn't deny that even narcissistic intellectuals can make important contributions to the human community. Nonetheless, they are mutilated persons who have deprived themselves of some of the greatest joys of life. For intellectuals whose work does not directly involve the human or social spheres, communication with other men is indispensable, not only for their personal fulfillment but for the efficacy of their work as well. I have often had occasion to observe that intellectual influence is rather directly proportioned to the emotional richness of him who wields it. Intellectuals who are imprisoned in narcissism are not likely to make a significant impression. Some of them are so contemptuous of others that they are not even concerned with the influence of their writing or teaching. They are content to proclaim what they take to be the truth and resign themselves to the fate of unheralded geniuses, all the while accusing others of being too dull witted to understand them. Many such intellectuals border on paranoia.

# 7

# *Intellectual Women*

Most intellectuals are men, although history records the existence of female scholars in all ages. By inviting writers, philosophers, and other intellectuals to their literary salons they often played an important role in the intellectual life of their times, served as catalysts for many currents of ideas, and inspired numerous masterpieces. But with rare exceptions they were not genuine intellectuals. They were often intelligent and keenly interested in the things of the mind, although generally more emotionally than intellectually motivated. We must admit too that many, particularly the *précieuse,* were attracted to literature or philosophy because it was fashionable.

But this does not mean that women are incapable of real intellectual endeavor, although it is widely thought that they are too superficial and emotional to be capable of objective reflection. The reason why there have been so few women intellectuals in the past, and why they are still a minority, is less the presumed inability of women than the psychological and sociological conditions they lived under. Not so long ago

women were barred from higher education. Girls were educated in their homes, the convent, and later the public
schools along practical lines. They were primarily destined to
be wives, mothers, and homemakers. Whatever culture they
acquired was purely ornamental, intended, so to speak, to
sweeten social conversation. It is astonishing, and speaks well
for woman's intelligence, that even under these conditions
some succeeded in becoming genuine intellectuals.

The condition of women has probably changed more in
the last fifty years than in the thousand preceding years.
Today women in the West are admitted to the same schools
and intellectual professions as men. There are women professors, doctors, lawyers, writers, and even scientific researchers.
Nonetheless, certain prejudices persist. It is still generally
thought that woman's real vocation is marriage and mother-
hood, while studies and professional activity are looked upon
as provisionary occupations or, in some cases, security against
possible spinsterhood. Consequently many girls, some of
them highly gifted, are not as serious about their intellectual
formation as men and compete poorly with them. I think
this, rather than some supposed natural inferiority, explains
why genuine intellectuals among women are still relatively
rare although their numbers are increasing.

## THE FEMALE INTELLECTUAL
## AND LOVE

There is no doubt that women have the right, indeed the
duty, to develop their intellectual capacities. As much as men
they should fructify their talents for their own fulfillment as
well as the good of the human community. But they also have

the right and the duty to develop emotionally. It appears that their need and capacity for love is appreciably greater than man's, and I do not believe this is uniquely because of their education or the conditions of life which are imposed on them. It follows, therefore, that the harmonious development of mind and heart is more important for women than for men. That it is often difficult to achieve such harmony may readily be granted, but the difficult is far from being synonymous with the impossible.

Many feminists and antifeminists agree on one point: the intellectual woman should never marry. Antifeminists think of the intellectual woman as a kind of monster. She is pictured as a cerebral termagant without warmth, not only unsuited to home life but incapable of love as well. She is usually suspected of being a lesbian. As for the feminists, many of whom are intellectuals in their own right, they know they are capable of loving and claim the right to do so. Some of them are of the opinion that the desire for marriage and children is a simple consequence of the education they received as young girls. In the present state of mores, this constitutes an inhibition to woman's intellectual fulfillment that is difficult to overcome. Thus it is normal for the ordinary woman to marry and have children while the intellectual woman should renounce domestic responsibility. Feminists, of course, do not ask the intellectual woman to give up love or sexual pleasure but advise her to avoid commitment or family obligations. This position is the more acceptable today, since scientific progress is well on its way to making procreation a matter of free choice. Christian feminists, who also exist, share most of their colleagues' premises, but morality prohibits them from endorsing free love; they urge instead sublimation of the sexual instinct and say

that the intellectual woman should seek her emotional fulfillment in the practice of charity.

In discussing intellectuals of the male sex in the preceding
chapter we omitted our opinion that the most "cerebral"
among them would be well advised not to marry—for their
own good as well as that of others—unless they first of all
obtain release from their inhibitions and repressions through
therapy. The same advice holds, perhaps more so, for certain
intellectual women. Experience has proven that women are
generally more exclusive than men and are less capable of
compromise. Some women intellectuals give themselves to
their profession with such passion that scarcely any energy is
left for the demands of family life. I do not contest the fact
that woman has the best chance of realizing herself in
conjugal love. But no one today would deny that there are
other roads to fulfillment as well. In former times it was
altogether natural for large numbers of women to enter the
convent; they were not for that reason considered diminished persons deserving of pity. Why not, by the same token,
admit that in our secular society highly educated women can
find fulfillment in an intellectual vocation. There is something laughable and unjust in the middle-class habit of giving
precedence at a dinner to a young married woman of twenty
over a forty-year-old celibate, even if the latter be an eminent
professor or a celebrated writer. We can only approve the
custom that is being more and more accepted of addressing
mature women as "Madame"; there is in fact something
pejorative implied in "Miss" except in the case of very young
girls.

But celibacy is by no means a moral obligation for women
intellectuals. They have the right, as much as men, to the
emotional fulfillment that family life brings. Many women

have in fact successfully combined a successful career with a family. I even know women actively engaged in politics who honorably acquit themselves of their duties as wives and mothers, although with greater difficulty in this case. This calls for great energy and resourcefulness.

## PROFESSIONAL LIFE AND HOME LIFE

For most female intellectuals some form of professional life seems indispensable to their fulfillment. They would feel that something were missing, even in the most successful of marriages, if they did not engage in the kind of life their studies prepared them for. I know a woman with a doctorate in philosophy who married a diplomat and had to give up teaching. At first she took great pleasure in her new life. But it only lasted a few years. A feeling of having been unfaithful to her vocation, of having failed in her life, became so obsessive that she sought recourse in therapy. Only after she went back to her professional work did she regain her emotional serenity and zest for life.

Other women intellectuals can give up their profession without any serious consequences. Helen, for example, was a superiorly gifted girl and did brilliantly in her literary studies. She was destined for a successful career as a university teacher and writer. But as soon as she finished school she fell in love with Louis and married him a short while later. In the beginning she tried to combine two careers. But her husband's social position entailed great responsibility, and she had several children one after the other. She was forced to give up her work and become a housewife. She resigned from her profession with some misgivings, very conscious of the painful sacrifice she was making. But she has continued to be an authentic intellectual. Better educated than her husband, she contributed greatly to his development and was in no small part responsible for his professional and social success. Her presence at social gatherings was always enriching for the other guests. When her children grew up she returned to educational work. She was also active in various organizations. Thus she made a number of creative contributions to her community. But not all women intellectuals have her health, maturity, and initiative. Still, her example is worthy of imitation. She at least proved that a married woman is not condemned to intellectual sterility. Again, one of the best-known woman novelists in France is a mother of a large family. Another woman intellectual of my acquaintance married an editor and shares actively in his work.

But let us now consider the case of a woman intellectual who marries and whose profession, although very fulfilling for her, cannot easily be reconciled with her husband's situation. Must she resign from her position? Under the present conditions of society this is generally what happens. When Agnes married at thirty-seven she was a well-known lawyer in a large city, a municipal counsellor, and an outstanding citizen of the community. She fell in love with and married an obscure notary public from a small town. Since both could not continue in their professions would it not have been objectively more normal for the husband to give up his? Agnes in fact proposed this. He hesitated, seemed to consent, then changed his mind and asked her to renounce everything. He said he would be ashamed to live off his wife. This is an illustration of one of those taboos, those persistent prejudices that must at all costs be overcome, since it is no longer in conformity with the situation of educated women. Objectively, there is no valid reason why man should be the head of the household. We are not arguing for a matriarchy such as seems to be emerging in the United States of America. Each case should be considered separately. In one intellectual family I know the woman, who is a doctor, earns the living. The husband is a talented composer but has not yet succeeded financially. But he is not embarrassed by the situation nor does he feel inferior to his wife. Today, there is no longer any reason to equate domination with earning money. Of course the same is not true in the case where a husband who is incompetent or lazy is being kept by his wife. Inevitably such a man will lose the respect of his family and of society at large.

## THE CHOICE OF A HUSBAND

The birth of love between two people is mysterious and often inexplicable. The question of what kind of man a woman intellectual should marry is therefore largely theoretical. But what we have to say may be of some help to those who have not yet fallen in love or who are hesitant about marriage.

The first question that might be asked is the following: should a woman intellectual marry someone with a similar background? In my experience a marriage between a woman intellectual and, say, a businessman is rarely satisfactory. The criteria of judgment and value as well as the interests of the two parties are likely to be too divergent. A businessman naturally attaches great importance to material success, seeing in it the confirmation of his own worth and that of others. Circumstances oblige him to socialize with other businessmen whose wives are not by any means all intellectuals. Conversation in such circles is much more likely to be about automobiles and horse racing than books or painting. On the other hand, intellectuals are as a rule not much at ease with either business or businessmen.

When Isabel married Marcel, a well-known fabric dealer, she was still a student. But her tastes were already explicitly, indeed exclusively, intellectual. She and her friends aspired to become writers, artists, professors, and scientists. She consented to marry Marcel because she was strongly drawn to him physically; in addition, she wanted release from the restrictive atmosphere of her own family. Marcel offered her a socially assured position free from material need. The first months of married love were ecstatic. She bought all the clothes and jewelry she wanted; they entertained extensively, and Isabel took great pleasure in her intellectual superiority to her husband's friends and particularly their wives. But her pleasure was short lived. She became more and more frustrated for lack of intellectual communication and could not help comparing her present situation to that of her former friends, now idealized by separation from them. She grew more and more nervous and depressed, to the point where life with her husband became intolerable, even though she recognized his kindness and love for her. She lost interest in entertaining her husband's friends; this in turn hurt him professionally and led to frequent arguments between them.

Marriage between colleagues is frequent among teachers. They know one another at a university, follow the same program of studies and lead the same kind of life. This gives them much in common and enhances mutual understanding. The principal disadvantage to this kind of marriage is the difficulty of avoiding monotony. The husband and wife have few contacts outside of educational circles and tend to converse too exclusively about their students and colleagues. The husband and wife should at least be in different fields. Otherwise they are tempted to make comparisons that are far from conducive to marital accord. If they teach different subject matter they can more easily safeguard a minimum of personal autonomy.

It is more important for a woman than a man to marry someone she can communicate with on the intellectual level. A man can usually make up for lack of intellectual exchange with his wife through his profession. But this is almost always more difficult for a married woman. She has too many commitments in the home, especially when the children are young. If she cannot communicate intellectually with her husband she is doomed to frustration. This is especially true if she is not engaged in any professional activity. Her infrequent contacts with the outside world can rarely fill the void in her life.

## RELATIONS OF FRIENDSHIP

However excellent the understanding and communication between a husband and wife, an intellectual woman cannot be happy as her husband's shadow. She must feel that she is an autonomous person and have activities and friends of her own. Of course, there is no reason why a couple cannot have the same friends, as is often the case in practice. But there is frequently some sort of incompatibility between a man's wife and his friends and vice versa. In such cases is compromise the best course to follow? By way of an answer to this question let me cite the case of a couple I knew very well.

Both the man and his wife were equally interested in intellectual matters and they were deeply in love with one another. But not all of their interests coincided. He was a doctor and had a mystical tendency that led to a keen interest in

Hinduism, yoga, and theology. He had many friends among the clergy and others who like him were seeking metaphysical and metapsychological truth. She had a more positivistic temperament and was more interested in social and political questions than in her husband's mysticism. In accordance with middle-class customs, they believed they should only go out together, spend time with the same people and frequent the same places. The outcome of this arrangement was predictable. He felt he was wasting his time at political rallies and lectures and resorted to sulking as a means of revenge. She found her husband's friends and their conversation terribly hard on her nerves. Even though they were exceptionally endowed for mutual understanding they quarreled more and more frequently. As their friend and confidant I advised them to change their social habits and pursue their interests independently of one another. The result of this new style of life led to a better understanding between them and also a greater interest in one another's activities. Since they no longer felt constrained each enjoyed greater personal autonomy. Dialogue between them became as lively as it was in the early days of their marriage.

This example won't work in all cases. But it is an indication of how an important existential problem that confronts many married couples can be solved.

I don't think there is any doubt that the female intellectual has as much need for friendship as a man, perhaps greater. Most of them have a special need for male friendships. When they marry they hope to find in love everything that could be expected of friendship. Among intellectuals, marriages often take place between friends and not infrequently the friendship continues long after age or routine has stemmed the fires of passion. Still, conjugal friendship is rare enough for a woman intellectual. Sooner or later she will want to break with the routine of domestic life and enjoy the kind of stimulation that can only be found with those whose interests are broad and informed. There can be genuine friendships among women. There is no question about that, popular prejudices notwithstanding. But a woman, particularly if she is not married, would be unduly stifled without the complementarity that comes from communication with members of the opposite sex. Teachers in schools where the faculty is entirely comprised of women often complain of the lack of contact with men who could broaden their intellectual horizons. Their decision to join a mixed faculty is not always motivated by the desire to find a husband; it can be much more naturally explained as the more or less conscious need to meet male partners in dialogue.

## HOMEMAKERS

Intellectual women are often caricatured as poor homemakers because they are much more interested in books than cooking or children. I categorically deny the veracity of this image. It may be true of some but, I think, not many, and women who are not intellectuals can be equally poor housekeepers. By contrast some of the most competent homemakers I have ever met were intellectuals.

Gloria has a doctorate in philosophy, leads an active social life, is the mother of five children, and entertains frequently for her socially prominent husband. I know few homes that are better organized and few children who are better brought up. She manages to read difficult books in philosophy and theology and at the same time attend to her many household responsibilities. She and many others like her have often proved to be more efficient housekeepers than ordinary women. Because they are not so impressed with the importance of household problems they can resolve them more efficiently and with fewer dramatics. We can observe at all levels of life that those who are in varying degrees superior to a situation succeed best in confronting it.

# 8

# *Old Age and Retirement*

All things being equal, intellectuals resist the infirmities of old age better than most men. In his seventies, Teilhard de Chardin was still extraordinarily young in spirit. Instead of taking refuge in his memories and turning in upon himself as many old men do, he was still keenly interested in the future, including the distant future of mankind itself. He was up on all intellectual currents and very knowledgeable about the spiritual ferment that agitated the young. He shared fully their enthusiasm, so much so that the young were always perfectly at ease in his presence. When I came to know Henri Bergson personally, he was almost eighty years old. He did not have Teilhard de Chardin's robust physical health and was at the time quite ill; but what a marvelously youthful spirit! My editor and old friend, Fernand Aubier, bought and reconditioned a ruined castle when he was seventy-eight. He worked on the project as though he would enjoy it for long years to come. This man had spent his whole life almost exclusively with books; in his retirement he concerned himself with a thousand material tasks during the day. In the evening he reread the Greek classics. When death overtook him at the age of eighty-six, he was in the midst of translating several important works.

I could name a number of other intellectuals—some in good health, others rather sickly—who remained young at heart until they died. Is this not empirical proof that the spirit is far more than a mere function of the body? Bergson, for example, continued an intense intellectual life long after his body became infirm. It would seem to be a confirmation of the position, which Bergson had long held, that the soul will survive the body. Maurice Blondel, another great philosopher, wrote the five volumes of his masterpiece when he was old, physically exhausted, and almost blind.

## THE BOREDOM OF RETIREMENT

For intellectuals as for all men old age brings with it certain threats. The intellectuals we mentioned above overcame passivity to remain young in spirit until death; others of equal renown aged ungraciously. They withdrew into themselves, became bitter, pessimistic, and vindictive.

Writers, artists, and certain other intellectuals avoid the problems of age and retirement for the simple reason that they do not retire. Normally they remain active in their profession until their strength fails them. This is both an advantage and a disadvantage of the so-called "liberal" professions. Intellectuals of this kind can best withstand the dangers of old age by observing the general rules of hygiene we pointed out in earlier chapters.

But the situation is different for those intellectuals who are salaried—professors, researchers, engineers, psychologists, sociologists, doctors, and the like. Until the age of sixty or sixty-five they are principally occupied by their professional activities. Even their social life is conditioned by their profession. But convention decrees that at a certain age they must abruptly cease doing what had been so much a part of their lives. Some men, it is true, are really old and tired of working at that age and look forward to a well-deserved rest. Some members of officialdom continue to work only because of the attraction of retirement. The publicity for recruiting civil servants, for example, insists at great length upon this "advantage." But this mentality is rarely encountered among intellectuals. Almost all of them like their work and look upon it as a vocation, that is, as a justifying reason for their existence. Too, most intellectuals do not feel old at sixty or sixty-five, perhaps because they do not feel that their profession is a burden. In politics and certain private businesses there is no compulsory retirement age; quite the contrary, positions of the highest responsibility are generally conferred upon older men. There is something paradoxical in the fact that a Conrad Adenauer, for example, was chosen as chancellor of Germany when he was over eighty years old, while most men are considered too old to acquit themselves of far lesser responsibilities at sixty or even fifty-five years of age.

I have no intention of criticizing the laws that guarantee a minimum of security for old people. They are an incontestable sign of social progress. Retirement is also justified for the common good, for it makes way for younger people who are normally better able to understand the needs of the age. At the second Vatican Council there was a strong movement to set a retirement age for bishops, and however admirable some octogenarian statesmen may be they most often best serve their country by giving way to younger men. After thirty or forty years of teaching a certain weariness is bound to overtake even the most dedicated. The same is true of many other intellectual professions.

But retirement should not be synonymous with being put out to pasture, as though one were no longer capable of rendering any service to mankind. It should rather mark the beginning of a new life, a new creativity. Instead of being understood as a decisive step towards death, it ought to be desired as a new possibility. (We might note in passing that one of the reasons why religious faith has lost much of its attraction for modern man is because eternal life is seen as a kind of endless retirement, where one does nothing. Modern man views this as intolerable boredom.) This is applicable to everyone, but especially intellectuals. Those who earn their living by the sweat of their brow may well be ready for retirement at the age of sixty; indulgence in sports as well as gastronomy may indeed prove to be impossible after that age. But the same should not be true of those who, without disdaining the body and its pleasures, lived primarily for the joys of the spirit. The case of overwork excepted, intense activity rejuvenates rather than ages the spirit or at least prolongs its youth.

If the prospect of retirement is feared by many intellectuals it is because they lived too exclusively in terms of their professional activity and when this ceases they no longer know what to do with themselves. This is especially true of scientists, researchers, and scholars. From a characterological point of view, they are usually "secondary" types who resist change. They are often men of a single book or a narrow specialty. The complexity of modern science quite naturally encourages their penchant for excessive specialization. Few men of science had Einstein's breadth; he was not only an outstanding physicist but was equally interested in music and philosophy and fought for peace in the world and freedom for nations and individuals. I know a microbiologist who spent his whole life studying a certain kind of tropical flea. There is no doubt that he was an authority in his field; but he was interested in little outside of it. What could such a man conceivably do in retirement?

For teachers, clergymen, doctors, and men of action whose scope of awareness is generally broader than that of specialists, retirement also poses a number of psychological problems. Professional demands are often so absorbing that even with the best of will it is often difficult to take up some hobby or other. In the case of celibates, like priests and some teachers, it is altogether natural that all of their affection be directed to their parishioners or students. Their profession is their life. Retirement in their case is equivalent to not living. Those who had a lifelong habit of reading suddenly lose interest in it; people who were full of life while they were occupied succumb to depression, neurasthenia, and life-weariness. Attempts at suicide are not infrequent among people in retirement. But it is not necessary to commit suicide to hasten the advent of death.

Mrs. N. had taught history in a large high school for forty years. She was respected by her colleagues and students as much for her good teaching as for her fine human qualities. Her interests were all-encompassing. Many of her former students became in their turn history teachers. She frequently invited her better students to her small but comfortable apartment for an atmosphere more conducive to communication. When she reached the retirement age she was still as dynamic as many of the teen-age girls she taught. At first many of her former students came to see her, seeking advice about their studies and future vocations. But gradually life separated them from her and she became a mere name for the new students. Her life lost all meaning, all justification in her own eyes. She neglected her health and no longer did any housework. The pleasures of reading and going out faded. She became depressed and soon became a victim of neurasthenia. One day she was found dead in bed. A few years of retirement was enough to kill a woman who but a short time before seemed destined for long years of prolonged youth.

## THE REMEDIES

Is there any effective remedy against the dangers of retirement we have just analyzed? On one occasion when I spoke about this problem in a public lecture an elderly gentleman protested against the pessimistic impression I had given the audience. He said that he had never been so busy or lived so fully as during the five years he had been "enjoying" his retirement (he used the word deliberately). His testimony at least shows that retirement is no more doomed than any other age, that here as elsewhere the meaning of life depends in large part upon man's freedom. Old age and death are inevitable, but both can be retarded; man can view them either as utterly futile or as full of positive significance. A whole science of rejuvenation, associated with such names as Voronoff and Bogomoletz, has been progressively elaborated. The remedies they propose cannot be taken seriously if they are meant to camouflage the realities of old age—as is often done in "beauty institutions" and similar laboratories. But when the science of rejuvenation is based on a sound psychic and physical hygiene it merits our attention.

If retirement means the end of active life and the beginning of old age for so many of our contemporaries we must seek the explanation in the excessive importance they attach to work. This is more true of intellectuals than others because they tend to overidentify with their profession. Added to this is the increasing specialization in intellectual disciplines. As the necessary preparation to become a surgeon, economist, professor, or what have you becomes longer and longer, the chances of becoming familiar with fields outside the specialty decrease. Professional activity occupies our life so totally that when it ends we are at sixes and sevens and find it difficult to become interested in anything. I know many professional men who have never read anything serious outside of their field of interest. Even clergymen and professors, who in former times were considered widely read, today admit that they no longer have time to read anything other than what is required by the immediate demands of their work.

It is no part of my purpose to recommend a utopian return to "the good old days" before the pressures of modern technology invaded our lives. The remedy to the evils engendered by technological civilization must be found within that civilization. In the first place, a more extended and profound general education ought to precede specialized studies. The French custom of the bachelor's degree at seventeen or eighteen years old is absurd. In countries where the German influence predominates the equivalent examination takes place three or four years later, which perhaps explains the greater maturity of university students in those countries as well as their technological and economic superiority. The practice of introducing specialized studies at the secondary level is likely to let us in for some disagreeable surprises. The only effective countermove would be to restore general education to its place of honor and not begin specialization before the twentieth year. Nor is there any reason why courses of general cultural interest (archeology, languages, philosophy, or art) cannot be combined with specialized studies (in medicine, the physical sciences, or mathematics). Specialists would lose nothing by having a more broadly based education. Quite the contrary. The price paid by a few more years in school would be well worth it. Given the improved hygienic conditions and life-expectancy statistics today, the number of years dedicated to constructive work would not be appreciably diminished and the increased practice of financial assistance from government sources reduces the threat of another potential problem. In any case, specialists with a broad education will lead a far more interesting life and face retirement more optimistically.

But it isn't likely that reforms such as those we have sketched above will come about rapidly, for they presuppose an important change of mentality. It will take time to convince the public and legislators of their necessity. In the meanwhile we must be content with remedies that are, to be sure, very imperfect and depend for their effectiveness on individuals themselves.

Anyone who is convinced of the importance of maintaining his sanity and offsetting the boredom of old age and retirement absolutely must become interested in something outside of his profession. It is sovereignly important that we look upon retirement not as the end of real life but rather as a happy opportunity to consecrate ourselves to different occupations that we now have the time for. I have already cited several cases of men who have triumphed over old age in such a manner. Here are a few more.

Bernard was the director of an insurance company. In addition to his many and absorbing professional activities he was passionately interested in archeology, which he studied during vacations. When he retired at sixty-five he found great joy in pursuing his interest on a full-time basis. It was as though he had rediscovered his youth. Mark was an industrialist. When he turned his business over to his sons he offered his services to a private organization for aid to underdeveloped countries. He thus continues to live fully and make a social contribution. When Dr. M. retired from his clinic in Paris he retired to the small town where his family came from. He was elected mayor and naturally experienced neither the boredom nor the feeling of uselessness that plagues so many retirements. A former professor of philosophy became a dedicated apiculturist and something of an authority on bees. Retirement gave him an opportunity to indulge an interest he had always had.

It is my conviction that most intellectuals can be similarly creative in their twilight years. But it is important that they develop hobbies in early life. This is infinitely more likely to prolong their youth than all the drugs of "rejuvenation."

# 9

# *The Intellectual and Religious Faith*

When clerics were almost the only intellectuals in society the problem we intend to discuss in this final chapter did not exist. It was taken for granted that the intellectual was a man of faith. Albert the Great, Thomas Aquinas, Bonaventura, Meister Eckhart, and many others were both scholars and saints who explicitly placed their intellectual work in the service of the faith. Science and religion, far from being in conflict, were like two sisters engaged in mutually complementary enterprises. Science was readily proclaimed: *ancilla fidei,* the handmaid of faith. This changed with the Renaissance. Leonardo da Vinci and most other humanists continued to treat religious themes in their writing and art, but this was merely a concession to tradition. The humanistic mind, even in the case of priests and monks, was no longer in perfect harmony with the faith. Many in fact came close to professing atheism. During the Enlightenment of the eighteenth century, philosophers and their disciples taught that it was impossible for a thinking man to be a believer. It was understood that the intellectual should fight for scientific progress under the aegis of "light," while religion was considered obscurantist. Not so long ago it was a matter of course for a young man beginning his studies in philosophy, history, and the natural sciences to lose his faith. Further, those who were committed to social progress considered it their duty to break with religion. These views were shared by believers and unbelievers alike, which explains in part the Church's long-standing contempt for science and social movements.

I do not intend to discuss the validity of the intellectual's objections to religious faith. Today, in any case, the conflict is less intense. There are many philosophers and scientists in all specialties who openly profess the Christian faith and find support for their belief in their scientific investigations. Others, usually because of prejudices against the traditional religion of their country, turn to the religions of the Orient. The fact that these religions are more difficult to harmonize with science does not bother them; they argue that there is a place in the full human life for both science and religion and there is no need to reconcile them. Intellectuals who are unbelievers generally respect their believing colleagues and try to understand their position. Thus Roger Garaudy, the principal member of the Communist intelligentsia in France, recently declared: "Religion can be a leaven," a concession that but a short time ago would never have been made by a rationalist philosopher. Garaudy went further and questioned the classical Marxist theses on religion: "The Marxist conception of religion can be reduced to a single formula: religion is the opium of the people, as though religion were everywhere and always an obstacle to work, research and combat." Today it is generally admitted by intellectuals that atheistic or agnostic rationalism has not succeeded in procuring happiness and well-being for all men, that it is incapable in itself of clarifying all the problems and mysteries of existence. Believers for their part no longer look upon atheistic intellectuals as the devil's collaborators whose principal if not unique goal is the destruction of religion. They recognize with Pope John XXIII their own share of responsibility in the schism between Christians as well as movements of social and scientific progress. Intellectual ecumenism is one of the healthy signs of our times and constitutes a proof of the maturity of the contemporary intelligentsia. Depth psychology furnishes evidence that fanaticism and sectarianism, far from being a sign of firm conviction, indicate rather their fragility, the fear that they might be shaken as soon as we recognized that "others" can also be in good faith and share in the truth.

Because many prejudices on both sides have disappeared, dialogue between believing and unbelieving intellectuals is now possible. But it is far from easy for an intellectual to adhere to a religious faith and still more difficult to join a Church. In the time of Pasteur it was admitted that the intellectual could believe in God, profess all the dogmas of the Church and participate in its ceremonies and rites without trying to bring his belief into accord with his philosophical or scientific convictions. Today that kind of separation is impossible. To be sure, an intellectual who is also a Christian is so not because of any kind of rational proof but because the grace of God has enlightened him. He perhaps more than other believers knows that faith is in the final analysis a gift of God. Still, an intellectual would be unfaithful to his specific vocation if he did not try to understand what he believes. *Fides quaerens intellectum*, faith seeks understanding, as Augustine has said.

It is a well-known fact that Catholic theology, as it is

taught today in seminaries and the catechism, was elaborated in the eighteenth century. Since that time it has been little more than a commentary on the writings of the medievals. The key concepts in this theology are not biblical but were borrowed from Greek philosophy as it was known to the Middle Ages, principally through the intermediary of the Spanish Arabs. Thomas Aquinas, Duns Scotus, and other medieval theologians were not much concerned with the meaning these concepts had for Plato, Aristotle, or Plotinus. They were not historians and made no effort to understand philosophy in the context of Scripture or the patristic tradition. It was only later, under the influence of uninspired commentators, that words like "substance," "form," "accident," etc., acquired dogmatic rigidity. An intellectual of our times who reads St. Thomas without presuppositions or prejudices would be less shocked than if he read the later commentaries and particularly the seminary textbooks. No self-respecting intellectual today could embrace the latter.

Theology manuals and most catechisms present the dogmas of Christian revelation in such rigid formulas that one gets the impression that the physics and cosmology of the Greeks is still universally valid. What can the doctrine of hylomorphism, by means of which theologians try to explain the Eucharist and other sacraments, mean to anyone even superficially familiar with modern theories of matter? The case of John R. is illustrative in this respect. Shortly after his conversion to Catholicism he had a painful experience. Like most intellectuals educated in the pluralistic atmosphere of the university, he was not attracted to Christianity for dogmatic reasons. But once he had become a Christian he naturally made an effort to justify his decision intellectually. Thus he began a study in all good faith of theology as it is currently taught. Alas! What he read convinced him of nothing. The explanations of the Incarnation, Trinity, Redemption, Eucharist, and Creation bore no relationship whatsoever to his own philosophical and scientific knowledge. Ptolemy's cosmology, Aristotle's physics and scholastic syllogisms could at best have an historical interest, but they couldn't convince him. He was faced with this alternative: either reject religion in the name of intellectual honesty or opt for a blind faith. At that point a friend introduced him to the writings of Teilhard de Chardin, where he discovered a magnificent synthesis of the Christian faith and modern science.

Of course, one does not have to be a disciple of Teilhard de Chardin to make sense out of the Christian faith. John himself is not in agreement with many Teilhardian positions; but Teilhard's methodology and spirit are exemplary. He did not create a new system; but he did make it clear that no one is obliged to accept the faith blindly. Nor is it merely a question of a forced relationship between faith and science, as if religion could make up for the provisionary inadequacies of science. It is important for the educated man of this century to acquire a religious education comparable to his general education. Otherwise he will be a divided man. God, Teilhard wrote, is not the negation but the prolongation of the world. This phrase is a good indication of the direction the modern intellectual must take in his quest for religious intelligibility.

Gaston is a well-known young physicist. He maintains that he is quite happy to practice the simple faith he learned from his mother, who died when he was an adolescent. He is a fervent practitioner; like his mother he makes novenas, goes to communion on the first Friday of the month, and wears a scapular medal. He refuses to join study clubs that explore the implications of religion in greater depth. He is an admitted conservative in the sense that he accepts the whole repository of traditon without question, which is to say, without making an effort to understand it. The *aggiornamento* of Vatican II shattered his simple faith. The Council fathers had in fact questioned many of the "traditions" which Gaston and others like him identify with Tradition. Mass was now said in the vernacular in his parish church. The Protestants were looked upon favorably, although he had learned from his mother that it was a sin to play with boys of the Reformed faith. John XXIII extended a friendly hand to atheistic Communists. In sum, Gaston no longer recognized his mother's religion and saw no reason to continue going to Church. His case is typical of certain educated Christians' refusal to harmonize faith and intelligence.

Many of the basic dogmas of Christianity, like the Trinity, the Incarnation, and the Eucharist are much more easily understood in light of modern science and philosophy than in the perspective of a static philosophy and a substantialist physics. Thanks to Teilhard de Chardin, John (mentioned above) could interpret creation in evolutionary terms and understand the "real" presence in the Eucharist as a form of energy. Now such matters make sense to him whereas previously he felt he had to believe *quia absurdum*. And Teilhard's insights by no means exhaust the ways in which the tenets of faith can be made intelligible. The important thing for all intellectuals is to bring their faith into the greatest possible harmony with their intellectual convictions. Thus one could be convinced that evolution is no longer a hypothesis but a definite scientific certitude and still admit that a philosopher of a different persuasion could contest this certitude. On the other hand, it would be intellectually dishonest to be an evolutionist in science and reject evolution on the religious level.

Many intellectuals today call themselves "spiritual men." Some fancy that they are very close to Christianity. The greatest obstacle in their way, they argue, is the Church. With its authoritarian organization, its discipline, its pomp and ritual, the Church seems terribly anachronistic and in contradiction with the deepest aspirations of the modern world.

Their position is understandable. Intellectuals within the Church admit that such criticisms are justified. Their books are often condemned for the most opportunistic of reasons. They suffer from the ridiculousness of ecclesiastical pomp, the puerile vanity that many members of the hierarchy affect in both their dress and mentality. If they remain faithful to the Church it is because they are convinced that the essence of faith has nothing to do with such superficialities. They view the Church as the community of believers or, better still, the community of all those who work for the advent of the kingdom of God even if some of them interpret this biblical image in terms of human fraternity and a better life in this world. For such intellectuals there is no doubt that the Church must and can adapt herself to the mentality of the modern world.